THE STARS OF FOOTBALL

THE STARS OF
FOOTBALL

THE WORLD'S BEST PLAYERS

RODOLPHE GAUDIN

GELDING STREET PRESS

A Gelding Street Press book
An imprint of Rockpool Publishing

PO Box 252
Summer Hill
NSW 2130, Australia

www.geldingstreetpress.com

ISBN: 9781922662187

Original French edition *Les Etoiles du Football* © Larousse 2024

This edition published in 2024 by Rockpool Publishing
Copyright design © Rockpool Publishing 2024

Cover photo credits, from left to right:
HAALAND – Bildbyran/Icon Sport;
MESSI – Estadao Conteudo/Icon Sport;
BENZEMA – Philippe Lecoeur/FEP/Icon Sport;
MBAPPÉ – Icon Sport

Other photo credits listed on p. 198

Publisher: Luke West, Rockpool Publishing

Adapted to English by Russ Gibbs
Edited by Lisa Macken

NATIONAL
LIBRARY
OF AUSTRALIA

A catalogue record for this
book is available from the
National Library of Australia

Printed and bound in China

10 9 8 7 6 5 4 3 2 1

CONTENTS

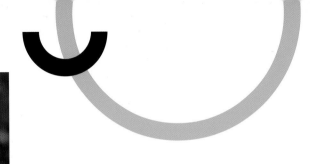

INTRODUCTION

The *Stars of Football* profiles more than 90 players, telling the stories of their rise to prominence and major successes. The book is packed full of anecdotes about the biggest names from the elite club leagues and the World Cup . . .

. . . and what a World Cup it was in Qatar, with so many emotions! It was ultimately a cruel campaign for France: Kylian Mbappé's gang did not deserve to lose the final via a penalty shootout, but one nation had to lose. Conversely, Leo Messi's Argentina hit the jackpot, Doha becoming the venue for this genius's long-awaited coronation and giving Argentina their third World Cup and their first since 1986.

For this edition you will discover new stories and extraordinary tales of destinies achieved. The profiles in this book will explain how the lives of many football geniuses changed and evolved and also serve as models of success for all aspiring footballers. As I've seen many times, while the miracle recipe does not exist, those who chase their dreams and work on their skills on a daily basis will find success. Our champions all speak the same language to get to the top regardless of from where they hail.

I think this 2024 edition of *The Stars of Football* is tastier than ever. It features a batch of young players who have quickly established themselves as popular heroes, from the Georgian pearl Khvicha Kvaratskhelia to Enzo Fernández, the revelation of the last World Cup.

Every year football offers us several such players heading for superstardom. In this book you will learn of their singular journeys and the adversity they have overcome to reach the top. In most cases these exciting talents soon gravitate to the powerhouse clubs of Europe, much as fans do. Chances are your favourite club is well represented over the following pages.

I hope you enjoy *The Stars of Football*, a book published in France for many years as *Les Etoiles du Football* and now, excitingly, available in English.

Rodolphe Gaudin

David

ALABA

BORN: 24 June 1992
Vienna, Austria

HEIGHT: 1.80 m

POSITION: Defender

PROFESSIONAL CAREER:
Bayern Munich,
TSG Hoffenheim,
Bayern Munich,
Real Madrid

Never in trouble as a youth, it was only when he was playing football that David Alaba refused to listen to authority. When his father George asked him to come home to the dinner table the little Alaba continued to play with his Viennese friends; otherwise, at school and in his everyday life the boy was a perfect role model.

The first black person to complete his military service in the Austrian army, George Alaba educated his children with the principles of respect. Unsurprisingly, David's father also sacrificed much for his son to succeed. As a youngster David was driven to and from training at Aspern SV by George, the father recovering in the family's old Ford Escort while David was learning the ropes on the pitch.

At the age of 13, David left the family nest for the Stronach Akademie, the training centre of Austria's Vienna. The following year he was spotted during a match in Tyrol by the famed Bayern Munich scout Werner Kern. Arriving in Munich, David initially found his integration tricky. The mentality at the German giant was hard to get used to, the Bavarian club arriving at tournaments spectacularly dressed in the official club tracksuit and in the most beautiful coach. Above all, Bayern always seemed to walk away with the trophy!

It was this culture of winning that Alaba learned over time, imposing himself on the team and earning a place in the first team as a rampaging left back, becoming known in the Rhine region as the 'complete footballer' – a nickname that was coined even before he was a regular in the dominant Bayern squad, then under the tutelage of Louis van Gaal.

Under the Dutch boss Alaba was a mainstay in the side for more than a decade, enjoying his time on the flank. With the talented French international Franck Ribéry placed in front of him, the duo became firm friends both on and off the field. In this Bayern juggernaut, Alaba won a multitude of prestigious titles.

In October 2009, at just 17 years and 3 months old, he became the youngest international in the history of Austrian football, making his debut in a 1–3 loss to France at the Stade de France in Paris. And he continues to write his success story, scooping the La Liga title and the Champions League in his first season at Real Madrid following his transfer from Bayern. Now that's what we call making your mark!

ALABA

DID YOU KNOW?

When you are from Austria it is impossible not to be a ski fanatic. In the land of the kings of sliding, David Alaba is no exception. The left-sided player is a particular fan of Marcel Hirscher, several times champion of the downhill world. And when winter spreads its white coat over the Tyrolean peaks, David Alaba turns into an attentive spectator, especially in Kitzbühel, the temple of the sport.

SPAIN

Thiago
ALCÂNTARA

BORN: 11 April 1991
San Pietro Vernotico, Italy

HEIGHT: 1.74 m

POSITION: Midfielder

PROFESSIONAL CAREER:
FC Barcelona,
Bayern Munich,
Liverpool FC

Thiago Alcântara fell into his vocation when he was just a child, a ball never being far from his feet. His father Mazinho was world champion with Brazil in 1994 and his brother Rafinha plays with Paris Saint-Germain (PSG), so football is very much in his blood.

Thiago Alcântara was born in southern Italy when his father was playing for US Lecce, but it was in his adopted country of Spain that he grew up. He also made regular trips back to his father's homeland of Brazil, where Thiago was able to sharpen his technique at giants Flamengo, the great Carioca club. However, when his father moved to Celta Vigo, Thiago, by then a promising young midfielder, began to anchor his playing style in the same way as the Galician club.

While Spain is significant to Thiago's development, his adolescence was spent in the prestigious surrounds of La Masia, the historic FC Barcelona Academy. Thiago is an eclectic mix of both Brazilian and Spanish background. 'My style, I don't just owe it to Barça,' Alcantara recalled. 'There are also inspirations of Brazil in my pivotal role. The Blaugrana gives you the game philosophy. The rest you learn on the job.'

After growing up with the Catalan cadets Thiago found himself training with the Barcelona professionals. His rise was noticed by Chelsea, who made great efforts to lure him to London, but Pep Guardiola watched over his young prodigy. Then in 2008 Luis Enrique accelerated his inclusion into the first team set-up.

At international level Thiago could have chosen one of three countries – Brazil, Italy, or Spain – but opted for La Roja. He made his debut in 2011, ironically claiming a first cap against Italy in Bari, the region of the country he was brought up in. Later that year he found himself established in the Barcelona jersey alongside his younger brother Rafinha.

After a successful spell at Barça, Thiago's next step saw him follow former coach Guardiola to Bayern Munich, signing for the German side in the 2013 off-season. Despite winning a multitude of titles at Bayern a series of injuries thwarted any further progress, and after being a part of the side that won seven Bundesliga titles in succession Thiago made the move to the English Premier League, signing for Liverpool. His time at Anfield has been tricky, but he did claim an FA Cup winner's medal in 2021/22 and has proven throughout his career that patience is one of his many virtues.

DID YOU KNOW?

On 20 September 2020 in the Premier League, during the match between Liverpool and Chelsea, Thiago Alcântara beat an incredible record. Entering the break, the midfielder had more passes – 75 in total – than any player in any other Premier League match in history. This was more than other players who have played 45 minutes or less in a meeting, since the Premier League was first analysed in 2003. The Reds won the match at Stamford Bridge 2–0.

ALCÂNTARA

Trent
ALEXANDER-ARNOLD

BORN: 7 October 1998
Liverpool, England

HEIGHT: 1.75 m

POSITION: Defender

PROFESSIONAL CAREER:
Liverpool FC

The blood that runs through the veins of Trent Alexander-Arnold is unquestionably a little redder than it is in most common mortals. This is because Alexander-Arnold, who is currently considered one of the best right-backs in the world, has been a loyal Red since he was six years old.

Very quickly, the young prodigy was spotted by Liverpool legend Steven Gerrard, who in his biography was effusive in his praise for a youngster who lit up the club's training base on a daily basis. In his book Gerrard wrote: 'Trent has a real chance of one day becoming a professional at a very high level, he has all the qualities for that.'

The Scouser was quick to prove himself worthy of the hopes of his illustrious elder. The lad, who once held Jamie Carragher's hand when he escorted the players as they entered the cathedral of Anfield, made his professional debut just days after blowing out the candles on his 18th birthday cake. It was October 2016 to be exact, and Tottenham Hotspur provided the opposition.

Much like the incredible turn of pace he showcased throughout his early displays, everything moved extremely quickly for Alexander-Arnold, and he capped his maiden appearance in the Union of European Football Associations (UEFA) Champions League in August 2017 with a special goal against the German side Hoffenheim. The following season he provided a record 12 assists in the Premier League, the most ever by a defender in the competition. A series of excellent performances saw him selected in the UEFA Best X.

Just a few months later, at 20 years old, he dethroned the Italian Christian Panucci to become the youngest player in history to play in two consecutive Champions League finals. These feats saw his reputation soar, the Golden Boy of the Reds being valued at a mind-boggling €100 million. This hasn't affected him, though, as the down-to-earth defender is seemingly impermeable to praise and has kept a cool head throughout, even retaining his shirt number of 66.

'We don't like to give them a little number in case they think they succeeded right away,' explained Lee Radcliffe, jersey management coordinator for Liverpool FC. 'For Trent, we chose this number because he was just coming out of the academy' – a number the star chose to retain despite his new status.

DID YOU KNOW?

Besides being an intelligent football player, Trent Alexander-Arnold is also passionate about chess. As a gift for his 20th birthday he met one of the absolute legends of the chessboard, Magnus Carlsen. The Englishman even allowed himself a small duel against the Norwegian, being swept away in 17 moves and five short minutes of play. As consolation he can always tell himself he outlasted Bill Gates, who was knocked out in just nine moves!

ALEXANDER-ARNOLD

GABON

Pierre-Emerick

AUBAMEYANG

BORN: 18 June 1989
Laval, France

HEIGHT: 1.87 m

POSITION: Striker

PROFESSIONAL CAREER:
AC Milan, Dijon FCO,
Lille OSC, AS Monaco,
AS Saint-Étienne,
Borussia Dortmund,
Arsenal FC,
FC Barcelona,
Chelsea FC,
Olympique de Marseille

An event in November 2016 perfectly summed up the character of Pierre-Emerick Aubameyang, a specialist in emotional uplift. Without warning the Franco-Gabonese striker decided, on the sly, to go and celebrate a friend's birthday in Milan. Taking a private jet, a lavish gift package and with cake and candles in hand, it wasn't long before photos began to circulate on social media. Unsurprisingly, all of this did not go down well with his then-club Borussia Dortmund's team boss, Thomas Tuchel, who sanctioned 'PEA' and banished him to the stands for the Champions League match with Sporting.

A week later the repentant star, who had been caught with his hand in the jam jar, was rehabilitated into the team and promptly slammed home a quadruple in a Bundesliga battering of Hamburg. Simply, Aubameyang is a paradox. He is the perfect example of an endearing guy, someone with a permanent smile who does not hide his attraction for the bling-bling style. Despite this taste for luxury and its atmospheric side, Aubameyang does not cheat in training. Never has a coach complained of his lack of involvement, appreciating the 100 per cent investment of this pure sprinter.

Aubameyang made a breakthrough at the highest level at AS Saint-Étienne (ASSE), quickly becoming a darling of the supporters of Les Verts. With this phenomenon in their ranks the Foréziens even won at the Parc des Princes against a strong PSG, and capped it all by winning a league cup in 2013: a title that had escaped ASSE for 32 years!

Despite being selected for the France U-21 team, Pierre-Emerick finally opted for the Gabonese jersey. He became captain of the Panthers and followed the path traced by his father. His involvement is always total; during the Africa Cup of Nations (CAN) 2012 he was reduced to tears after missing a penalty against Mali in the quarter-final shoot-out defeat.

Consolation came in the form of a transfer to Borussia Dortmund and then a move to Arsenal, where he became the most expensive Gabonese player in history (€63 million). At the end of the 2018–19 season, along with fellow Africans Sadio Mané and Mohamed Salah, PEA finished top scorer in the Premier League with 22 goals. A great craftsman, Aubameyang latterly played for Barcelona and Chelsea, moving to new club Olympique de Marseille for the 2023–24 season.

DID YOU KNOW?

It was following an astonishing misunderstanding that Pierre-Emerick Aubameyang signed his first professional contract at AC Milan in 2007. While his father Pierre Aubameyang was playing at La Triestina, Pierre-Emerick missed a plane at an Italian airport and came across the sports director of the Rossoneri, who confused him with George Weah! The two men sympathised, and the Milanese boss agreed to welcome the young footballer to Millanello. Fate did the rest.

AUBAMEYANG

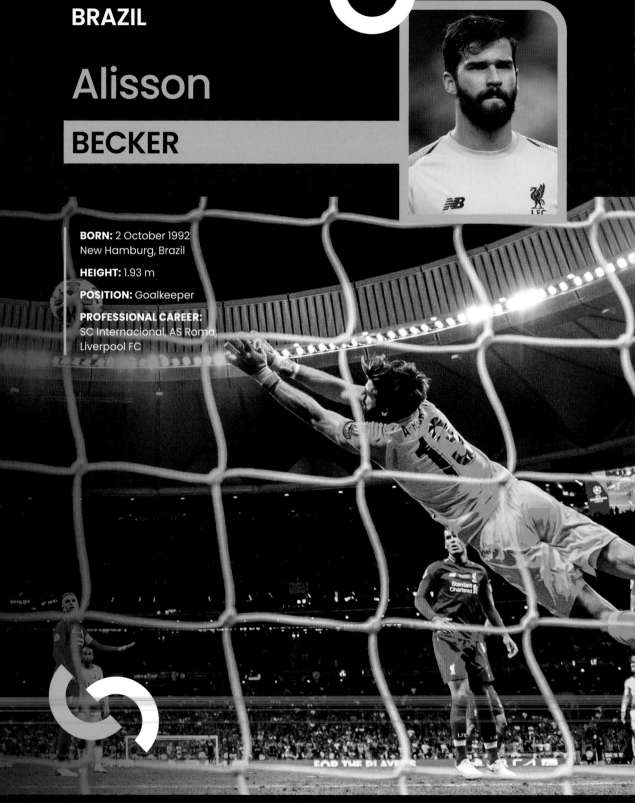

BRAZIL

Alisson

BECKER

BORN: 2 October 1992
New Hamburg, Brazil

HEIGHT: 1.93 m

POSITION: Goalkeeper

PROFESSIONAL CAREER:
SC Internacional, AS Roma,
Liverpool FC

He was the missing piece of the puzzle. In Kyiv on 26 May 2018, Liverpool lost 3–1 to Zinedine Zidane's Real Madrid in the UEFA Champions League final. For at least one of the goals scored by the Merengues, Reds' goalkeeper Loris Karius was held largely to blame. It thus became a priority for the club to recruit one of the best shot stoppers in the world, and two months later the English club took out its chequebook and signed Alisson Becker from the Eternal City: Rome. At a cost of €75 million the former AS Roma goalkeeper became the most expensive custodian in history.

What do you get for that price? A modern, complete goalkeeper who is half rock, half feline and always effective. For his first season in the Premier League Alisson made Reds fans very happy, going 20 matches without conceding a goal and more than one match in two with a clean sheet, which underlied his importance to the team. However, if there is one area where Alisson really impresses it's on his line.

Standing at 1.93 m tall, his impressive frame makes him excellent in the air, but he also has the agility and athleticism to get down to low shots. This combination, allied with some perfect positional sense, makes him the nemesis of opposition strikers. His uncanny reflexes from shots near and far are vital to the Liverpool cause. Just ask Lionel Messi and FC Barcelona!

Within 13 months the Catalan club had suffered two terrible defeats in the Champions League, nightmarish evenings that had one point of reference: Alisson Becker. Both times, in the second leg of the ties at the Stadio Olimpico and at Anfield respectively, Becker was an impassable wall who made all the difference. On two consecutive occasions he put an end to the Argentine number 10's dream of success in a fifth Champions League.

Goalkeeper for his international team since 2015, the Seleção number 1 really justified his huge fee in the final of the most important European competition, the Champions League. In the last quarter of an hour he pulled out two huge saves against Tottenham Hotspur, preserving Liverpool's lead. Madrid, on 1 June 2019, forever became Alisson Wonderland as Liverpool claimed their sixth cup with 'Big Ears'.

DID YOU KNOW?

Transfer discussions between AS Roma and Liverpool over the signing of Alisson had been intense and everyone had heard about it – enough for almost namesake Alison Becker to have fun on social networks. 'Very excited to announce that I will be joining Liverpool as a goalkeeper,' the American actress tweeted. The day after, Liverpool confirmed the signing of their new goalkeeper.

BECKER

Jude

BELLINGHAM

BORN: 29 June 2003

Stourbridge, England

HEIGHT: 1.86 m

POSITION: Midfielder

PROFESSIONAL CAREER:
Birmingham City,
Borussia Dortmund, Real
Madrid

The tearful farewell: in May 2023 Jude Bellingham found himself distraught, collapsed on the turf of Signal Iduna Park, Borussia Dortmund's cauldron of a home venue, inconsolable like everyone wearing yellow and black on that fateful day. While a ninth German championship title was within reach of the Schwarzgelben, the match scenario against Mainz for the last day of the Bundesliga turned into a nightmare. A 2–2 draw was not enough for Dortmund, who watched on as Bayern Munich stole the trophy out from under their noses with a last-minute winner in Cologne that saw the Bavarian giants retain their crown. For his last match in the Ruhr after three seasons, the young English midfielder obviously dreamed of an exit through the front door, garlanded and honoured. Apart from a German Cup, his time with the club remained empty of major titles. The film of his season must have paraded at high speed through his mind as the title slipped from his and his team's grasp.

It continued a season of enormous frustration for Bellingham, England having been beaten in the quarter finals of the 2022 FIFA World Cup by eventual runners-up France – this despite Bellingham being one of the stars of the entire tournament. On the stages of Al-Bayt in Al Khor Bellingham rose to the occasion, 'Jude Ball' releasing the full range of a complete player. He was a perfect bend of modern midfield dynamo, recovering the ball countless times, breaking opposition defensive lines with impunity and bringing danger to the opposition goal in and around the penalty box.

This prodigy from the West Midlands in the United Kingdom had been vaunted as a box-to-box expert and has had the power to intensify his game and direct those around him by actions alone. Naturally, these qualities of Jude Victor William Bellingham had caught the attention of a raft of clubs: PSG, Chelsea and Manchester City were all touted as destinations upon his Dortmund departure, but it was Los Blancos of Real Madrid that won the race.

For a long time English football lacked true creators, but now they have the perfect midfielder: he brings huge offensive ability but does not skimp on defensive effort, which makes him one of the most complete players in his position and for his age. Often compared to David Beckham, Jude Bellingham has a few years ahead of him to in turn achieve comparable status. His dynamic start to life in the Spanish Capital has only fuelled the feeling that this will be a case of when, not if.

DID YOU KNOW?

Jude Bellingham has worn the number 22 on his jersey for a long time, and he owes it to clever calculation. Due to his versatility he can play as a number 4, but also as a number 8 or a 10. Add it up and you get 22! It was his father Mark who had the idea, to better symbolise the multiple roles of his gifted son, always at ease in the heart of the game whatever his position.

FRANCE

Karim

BENZEMA

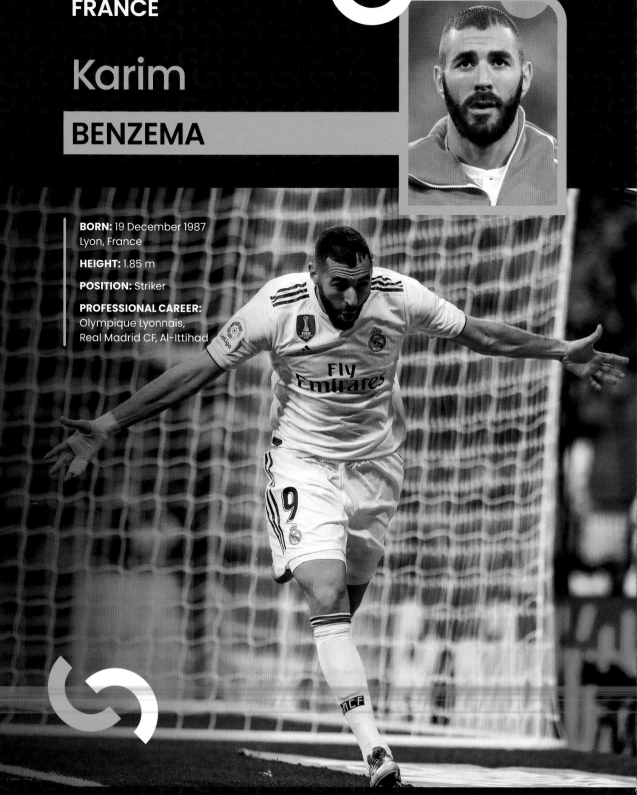

BORN: 19 December 1987
Lyon, France

HEIGHT: 1.85 m

POSITION: Striker

PROFESSIONAL CAREER:
Olympique Lyonnais,
Real Madrid CF, Al-Ittihad

When he arrived at Real Madrid in the summer of 2009 just before his 22nd birthday, Karim Benzema entered another dimension. In the Lyon bubble the young striker was impressive and a standout star.

Once in the workforce of the Merengues, a change of scenery for him, the young kid suddenly found himself thrust into the midst of a plethora of Galacticos. Nobody could have imagined then that during the next decade 'KB9' would plough his own furrow to become a legend in his own right. To last so long in such a club is testament to a foolproof adaptability and ability to bounce back at every moment.

Over several seasons the peak of his personal success was very much around Karim's agreement with Cristiano Ronaldo. While the Portuguese brought goals and glamour to Real, the child of Bron was Ronaldo's model teammate during those golden seasons when they won four Champions Leagues together.

Upon arrival at Bernabéu 'CR7' spent most of his time on the left flank, leaving the point of the attack to the Frenchman. Then, over time, the Portuguese folded his wings, settling at the top of the pyramid and leaving it to Benzema to ensure support and move away from the penalty area. An altruistic player, the ex-Lyonnais never took offence and was quick to stifle media speculation. 'Stop saying that I sacrifice myself for Cristiano; it's nonsense!' a passionate Benzema stated loudly and clearly. 'I like to play, I like football. It's not complicated to understand.'

Until March 2016 Didier Deschamps also defended his striker against all odds, even though many doubted Benzema's abilities would be translated into the major events on the world stage. Convinced of his hotshot, the coach announced that 'All the countries envy him,' but the issues involving the player in the Valbuena affair later cooled the ardour of the boss . . .

. . . That was, until Euro 2020, when Benzema was finally called up to join the ranks of the French team and made a welcome return following a substantial number of goals at club level. To cap it all, Benzema then claimed the 2022 Ballon d'Or as the best player in the world. He joined the European exodus to Saudi Arabia for the 2023–24 signing for Al-Ittihad.

DID YOU KNOW?

Better than Thierry Henry! During the 2018–19 season Karim Benzema became the top French scorer in the Champions League, reaching the symbolic bar of 60 goals in the prestigious event. Overall, the Real Madrid striker has only three players left in front of him: Cristiano Ronaldo (121 goals), Lionel Messi (106) and Raúl (71). In December 2005 the native of Bron had scored his very first goal in C1 during a Lyon-Rosenborg fixture (2–1) played at Stade Gerland.

ITALY

Leonardo
BONUCCI

BORN: 1 May 1987
Viterbo, Italy

HEIGHT: 1.90 m

POSITION: Defender

PROFESSIONAL CAREER:
Inter Milan, Treviso FBC,
Pisa SC, SSC Bari,
Juventus FC, AC Milan,
Juventus FC, Union Berlin

To remain at the bedside of his sick son, Leo almost gave everything up; there was no question that his life and passion for football needed to take a back seat. Suffering from an acute infection in 2016, little Matteo was saved by the medical profession and his champion dad has since resumed his career with even more motivation than before.

In his early career Leonardo Bonucci often suffered swings in concentration during a match, a bad habit that earned him the less than flattering nickname of 'Mister One Dumpling Per Match': hardly a moniker that was to his advantage! Soon, however, Bonucci's maturity was reflected in his performances, and he became one of the best defenders on the planet. It wasn't always this way.

In his youth the kid from the Rome region of Lazio was more of a midfielder, but on signing for US Viterbese he took a step backwards on the pitch and began to impose himself at the centre of defence. His displays, which relied on a sense of anticipation, his excellent heading game, his determination in duels and his formidable ability to raise cleanly thanks to an above-average ball to foot technique led to a move to Inter Milan.

To toughen up 'Bonny' was sent out on loan to Treviso, Pisa and then Bari, all in Serie B, but when he was recruited by Juventus in 2010 his career took off. Alongside Andrea Barzagli and Giorgio Chiellini he formed the other BBC, a much more defensive unit than that of Real Madrid CF's Bale, Benzema and Cristiano but one that gave cold sweats to all the attackers of the Italian peninsula and across the continent.

Bonucci's rise to international stardom was equally rapid. After just 20 matches in Serie A he celebrated his first call-up in February 2010, pulling on the Italian shirt in a 0–0 friendly stalemate with Cameroon at the Stade Louis II Stadium in Monaco. Eight years later, on the occasion of his 78th cap, he was made captain of the national team.

After more than 350 appearances for Juventus, the veteran defender was informed he would not be part of the team's plans for the new season, opening the door to a fresh adventure in Germany. The Italian statesman penned a deal with Union Berlin, making his debut in the club's maiden UEFA Champions League campaign against Real Madrid.

DID YOU KNOW?

Perfect for building character! Even if, at the time, the anecdote was painful, as a teenager Leonardo Bonucci suffered the threats of an unscrupulous peer. 'I was 14 and he tried to extort me,' the Italian defender remembered. 'I managed to escape. The episode marked me because I understood that I had to grow. If this boy attacked me it was because he thought I was weak.' A salutary life lesson.

Eduardo

CAMAVINGA

BORN: 10 November 2002
Cabinda, Angola

HEIGHT: 1.82 m

POSITION: Midfielder

PROFESSIONAL CAREER:
Stade Rennais FC,
Real Madrid

Having barely played in Ligue 1, it was evident early on that Eduardo Camavinga would not be lingering long in the French top flight, and that was confirmed in August 2021 when Real Madrid came knocking to swoop for the talented midfielder. Since his first appearance with the Stade Rennais in April 2019, Camavinga has been amazing the football world. At a time when records are being swallowed up by the precociously talented Kylian Mbappé, we will probably have to make some space for someone who obtained their French naturalisation shortly before Christmas 2019. A native of Cabinda in Angola, Camavinga quickly became an object of desire for Les Blues.

Eduardo seems to have no limits; his maturity and calmness are amazing at such a young age. Bred in Brittany, this terrier found coach Julien Stéphan, who launched Camavinga's career at the age of 15, and his assistant Mathieu Le Scornet, who had spotted him at the Ploumagoar tournament five years earlier. The trio was reunited and confident this would be a win-win for all involved.

At 17 years and 35 days Camavinga became the youngest player to score with Rennes in the top flight since the post-war period when he struck against Olympique Lyonnais, breaking on the counterattack to score what proved to be the match-winning goal. His outstanding achievements at both ends of the pitch demonstrated the full extent of the possibilities of this young combatant.

He defends with ice in his veins in a crowded penalty area and then shows composure at the other end to deceive the opposition goalkeeper, bluffing and annoying throughout. Goodbye and thank you, signed Camavinga. But perhaps his greatest strength is surely to succeed in still surprising people who have known him for a long time.

During Camavinga's years at AGL Drapeau-Fougères and his training at Stade Rennes all his educators praised his talent and ability to adapt to the next level. The question is no longer whether he is already part of a group of precocious talents such as Yoann Gourcuff or Ousmane Dembélé, who left their mark on the history of Rennes. The answer is a resounding 'Yes'. It's Real Madrid who is the winner, the signing of Camavinga surely the prelude to more silverware to fill the trophy cabinet.

CAMAVINGA

ITALY

Federico

CHIESA

BORN: 25 October 1997
Genoa, Italy

HEIGHT: 1.75 m

POSITION: Winger

PROFESSIONAL CAREER:
ACF Fiorentina, Juventus FC

The perfect archetype of the modern striker, the young transalpine Federico Chiesa is the king of timing his penalty box entries. Able to carry around the whole front of the attack, he also positionally looks like a nine and a half. 'Technically, on the left flank, I can transplant towards the axis, while on the right I try to go along the sideline before delivering a decisive pass,' this child of the ball insisted.

A good dribbler, excellent on set pieces and with superb peripheral vision despite long being criticised for playing with his head down, 'Pepo' knows how to rectify any situation. In his blood the native of Genoa has champion genes, his father Enrico having been an international with the Nerazzurri from 1996 to 2001. Born in Liguria, little Federico nevertheless made his first steps in Tuscany, near Florence, where his dad slammed in goal after goal in the Viola jersey of Fiorentina.

It is moreover at Fiorentina that the youngster did the majority of his classes. A good student, 'Fede' Chiesa had an excellent attitude to his studies. At the same time as football, he attended the University of Florence. Before skipping ahead, though, it is fair to remember that Chiesa Junior started with the primavera of Fiorentina in August 2016 before being launched into the seething duels of Serie A by Paulo Sousa.

Despite some up and down performances Chiesa got along perfectly with Croatian striker Nikola Kalinić and Federico Bernardeschi. A few months later the valuable advice of Franck Ribéry in training also helped him progress.

After making his way through the Italian youth ranks, Roberto Mancini gave Chiesa his first cap in March 2018 against Argentina, a 0–2 defeat. Well aware of the talent of the new generation, the head coach turned Chiesa into one of his jokers in the pack, and he was named as part of the Team of the Tournament at the delayed Euro 2020, in which Italy emerged triumphant.

In October 2020 Chiesa's departure for Juventus raised as many hopes as doubts. The Turin giants invested more than €50 million in Chiesa and in the peninsula some find the investment excessive; however, the perfectionist quickly silenced all his sceptics. Chiesa has been an exceptional signing for the Old Lady, settling into the squad and performing at elite levels on a weekly basis.

CHIESA

DID YOU KNOW?

Twenty-two years apart, the legendary Italian goalkeeper Gianluigi Buffon won the Italian Cup with both the father and then with the son! In 1999, in the Parma jersey, 'Gigi' won the trophy alongside Enrico Chiesa against Fiorentina over two legs (1–1 and 2–2). With Juventus in 2021 the 2006 world champion conquered the Holy Grail again, climbing to the top step of the podium and taking up a position near Federico Chiesa after overcoming Atalanta 2–1.

Kingsley

COMAN

BORN: 13 June 1996
Paris, France

HEIGHT: 1.81 m

POSITION: Winger

PROFESSIONAL CAREER:
Paris Saint–Germain FC,
Juventus FC,
Bayern Munich

Don't make him say what he doesn't think, but the departure of the two veterans Arjen Robben and Franck Ribéry at Bayern Munich finally freed up some space. Admittedly, competition has never scared Kingsley Coman, but the Parisian often had to start from scratch to sneak into a well-established workforce.

The fault of myriad injuries that hampered his young career, while the boy had the ability and instinct to shine his evolution looks like a roller coaster. Despite his reserved nature his teammates in the changing room appreciate the Frenchman. Consider this quote from David Alaba: 'King has the potential to quickly become a world-class player. I have rarely seen a guy so fast with ball at the foot.' Coman's style, which is all-in power and velocity punctuated by dazzling feints, is a feast for the eyes.

After arriving in Bavaria in 2015, having discovered football abroad from the age of 18 with Juventus, Kingsley Coman crossed paths with five renowned coaches. If the first time with Carlo Ancelotti was not the easiest, the native of Guadeloupe found a certain calmness on the left flank after passing under the watch of Pep Guardiola on the Bavarian bench before flourishing under the charismatic Jupp Heynckes. The experienced and influential German technician placed him on the right track. 'In particular, I told Kingsley to raise the head before centring and, sometimes, be better at managing his efforts.'

Initially loaned to Bayern, the French international was relieved when the Roten executives exercised the purchase option two seasons later. This meant he could quietly settle in the family home in Starnberg, by the lake. It's clear that Coman loves the club and the area, and winning seven titles with the Bavarian giants indicates he hasn't rested on his laurels. He has mastered the game more along with the language of Goethe.

Faced with repeated physical problems in recent seasons, consistency is the key for Coman. The only thing to do to get over these setbacks is to come back, work and focus on himself. Hard knocks have allowed him to acquire the necessary maturity to get up and go again, and Coman has mastered that well.

DID YOU KNOW?

A product of the PSG training centre, Kingsley Coman almost never joined the Camp des Loges. He mentioned that, at the time a nine-year-old kid, he lived with his parents more than 60 kilometres away in Moissy-Cramayel in the south of Seine-et-Marne. That was simply too far! Educated at the Parisian school Yves Gergaud, despite the scepticism of its leaders Coman ended up convincing them that the gifted can achieve wonders. And, even if he couldn't attend all training sessions, the 'King' was firmly established every weekend in the team and lit up every game.

BELGIUM

Thibaut
COURTOIS

BORN: 11 May 1992
Bree, Belgium

HEIGHT: 2.00 m

POSITION: Goalkeeper

PROFESSIONAL CAREER:
KRC Genk,
Club Atlético de Madrid,
Chelsea FC, Real Madrid

Thibaut Courtois finished as the best goalkeeper in the 2018 World Cup according to the Fédération Internationale de Football Association (FIFA), claiming the Golden Glove award, but that was of little consolation to the giant Belgian as his team was sent packing at the semi-final stage, a victim of France's march to the title. Les Bleus won the last-four match 1–0. Courtois found it all hard to digest, his bitterness at the defeat doing the rounds on social networks.

As soon as the failure at Saint-Petersburg was confirmed the Limburger let loose, first in the media of his country: 'It was a frustrating game. France did not play. She only defended with eleven players behind,' was his curt assessment. Even more infuriating was that it was a defender, in this case Samuel Umtiti, who put an end to the Belgian dream from a set piece. The Flemish giant did not expect the slingshot that ensued.

We could almost forget that the doorman of Brée reacted hotly in the grip of disappointment. The day before the final, as France got set to play Croatia, Thibaut Courtois diplomatically corrected the situation. 'I'm sorry if I expressed myself a little loudly,' he said. 'At Les Bleus, I know Griezmann, Kanté. I wish them victory.'

Turning around, the number 1 from Quiévrain also realised that his Belgium team had played the same tactics in defeating Brazil in a memorable match. He was exceptional during the quarter final against the Seleção, achieving no less than nine saves that included the last breathtaking one in extra time, tipping away a curling shot from Neymar. Despite the Red Devils' rearguard action, no Brazilian deplored the Belgians' approach to the fixture.

On his line Thibaut Courtois has many admirers, his stature and ball retention sure under pressure and his anticipation and ability to get down low when necessary belying his 2-metre frame. Under the stewardship of the defensively resolute Diego Simeone at Atlético de Madrid and Antonio Conte at Chelsea, Courtois was a rock behind teams that set up in a defensive block. Today, even at a more open and fluid Real Madrid, the rampart of Limburg has lost nothing of his imposing presence.

DID YOU KNOW?

Rififi in the land of Tintin! After leaving his post as Belgian coach Marc Wilmots attacked the Courtois family, accusing the father, Thierry, of having revealed to the press some of his starting 11. 'I just have a problem when I finalise my selection at 6 pm and that at 6.15 pm it is made public. It means that a player has "sold" the selection. I learned that it was Thibaut's dad who did it.' Courtois' father and son have decided to file a complaint for defamation.

COLUMBIA

Juan
CUADRADO

BORN: 26 May 1988
Necoclí, Columbia

HEIGHT: 1.76 m

POSITION: Midfielder

PROFESSIONAL CAREER:
Independiente Medellín,
Udinese Calcio,
US Lecce, ACF Fiorentina,
Chelsea FC, Juventus FC,
Inter Milan

W hen the shots rang out little Juan Guillermo, then four years old, hid under his bed exactly as his parents had asked him to do in such a situation. It happened one day in 1992, in Necoclí, a town in the north of Medellín, where the echo of the bullets is the ambient noise. Juan Cuadrado had just lost his father, killed by guerrillas, and was left to rely on his mother, who worked in a banana plantation to ensure the education of her eldest son, who even then lived only by and for the ball.

The Cuadrados also had to pay the 8,000-peso monthly fee for the football school. It was a sacrifice, but Juan's mother wanted to snatch her little son from a life of misery and violence. She was convinced of it: football was his chance, his exit. 'Already, in my belly, he was kicking and very strong,' she said. 'And to teach him to walk, we had to put a ball in front of him.'

With a playful child's face and oddly plaited braids on his skull, the frail winger does not leave anyone indifferent in his native Colombia. Considered brilliant but too thin, Cuadrado struggled to convince recruiters and only started at the age of 20 at Independiente Medellín, but it was there that he suddenly flourished.

Constant changes of direction, acceleration, lightning strikes, nutmegging: he did everything instinctively and gave the impression of improvising football with each touch of the ball. His reputation began to reach the ears of the big European clubs. Manchester United was a fan but it was in Italy that Juan found his base, accompanied of course by his mother.

Purchased by Udinese Calcio in 2009, Cuadrado struggled to adapt to the transalpine climate and the tactical constraints of European football. His performances were grey, but when he was loaned to Lecce he regained colour. Transferred to Fiorentina the following year, he proved to be one of Calcio's best players and a centrepiece of the selection.

The speedy winger has moved on to the next stage of his career, swapping Turin for Milan and black and white for blue and black. Inter fans will now get to see his marauding runs: defenders beware!

DID YOU KNOW?

Cuadrado also has class off the field! The proof? He offered his jersey number to Cristiano Ronaldo. The Portuguese, transferred from Real Madrid to Juventus in Turin, has been synonymous with the number 7 almost since the beginning of his career and he intended to wear it for his new club. He didn't even have to ask: his new Colombian teammate, the wearer of this number at the Old Lady, was happy to pass it over as a sign of welcome.

Kevin

DE BRUYNE

BORN: 28 June 1991
Tronchiennes, Belgium

HEIGHT: 1.81 m

POSITION: Midfielder

PROFESSIONAL CAREER:
KRC Genk,
SV Werder Bremen,
Chelsea FC,
VfL Wolfsburg,
Manchester City FC

I t is a headache for a coach, albeit a welcome one, that this capable Belgian is able to play in all positions in front of a defence and beyond, but no manager has had cause to complain – apart from maybe José Mourinho – about the benefit of such a midfield wonder. Long underrated, Kevin De Bruyne is now seen as a formidable game winner. He has learned when to run and when to release, and has evolved into a world-class operator.

'I love it when he evolves into a fake number 10,' Eric Gerets, the former Belgian coach of Olympique de Marseille, said. 'He is both able to score and distribute decisive passes.' However, it wasn't all rosy in the garden of the Red Devils either. During Euro 2016 De Bruyne and the Walloon, Eden Hazard, tiptoed through the matches, with Belgium increasingly being put under the magnifying glass. A shame when you have such talents.

'We love to play together, even if some people think it's not possible,' Hazard, who was visibly offended at the accusation that the duo could not combine in the national team, said. 'I am convinced that we are compatible. I'm more of a percussion player; Kevin is able to create breaches, to hit from afar.'

The result was more convincing during the World Cup in Russia in 2018, with Belgium installed on the third step of the podium albeit with the usual complaints from the media. 'Are you going to talk to me about my position in selection until the end of my career?' an annoyed De Bruyne asked. 'I play where the coach asks me, for the good of the team. It is not a question of freedom, but of space!'

Since reaching his peak at Manchester City, the data is better defined with Pep Guardiola. Thanks to his ability to occupy all the positions of midfield and attack in the same match, 'KDB' is a bit like an extension of the magician Guardiola's brain. 'Kevin is one of the best players I have ever seen, because he knows how to do everything, absolutely everything,' Guardiola insisted. 'He is a stable guy who loves the game and lives for it. He is so smart! He understands everything right away. He goes fast and sees space better than anyone.'

With his unique ability to break the lines and deliver decisive passes, the sensation that is Kevin De Bruyne is clear: he's world class.

DID YOU KNOW?

Not many players have stood up to José Mourinho. When he returned to Chelsea in the summer of 2013 after his loan to Werder Bremen, Kevin De Bruyne did not allow himself to become fazed with the spiky attention of the Portuguese coach. 'He had said in the press that I was not making the effort in training,' De Bruyne commented. 'It's easy to say that when nobody's around to check since the meetings are on camera, but everyone knows I'm not like that.' Have some of that!

DE BRUYNE

Frenkie

DE JONG

BORN: 12 May 1997
Arkel,
The Netherlands

HEIGHT: 1.80 m

POSITION: Midfielder

PROFESSIONAL CAREER:
Willem II Tilburg,
Jong Ajax,
Ajax Amsterdam,
FC Barcelona

At ASV Arkel in the outer suburbs east of Rotterdam, where it all started for him, Frenkie de Jong was surprised to learn that his former coaches had, for a time, considered using his first name on a tribune of their small stadium. The interested party refused on the pretext that he had not yet accomplished anything as a footballer.

Maybe not yet, but the strategist is no longer a stranger to the football world and especially since his international debut – which coincided with the return to the forefront of the game for the Netherlands, who had been plunged in mothballs for a few months – and also since his exploits with Ajax and, above all, his sensational transfer to FC Barcelona.

After a head-to-head showdown with PSG over the acquisition of de Jong, Barça won the bidding with a contract for five seasons. The amount of the operation was €75 million, plus €11 million in bonuses. The French world champions discovered de Jong's class one evening in autumn 2018 when they stalled in front of so much genius. 'I was going to hurry him, but I never managed to get near him,' Antoine Griezmann summarised.

Excellent with the ball, the pillar of the renewed Oranje is one of those players who spends the most time looking to play forward. Whether it be the long game or the short game, everything seems easy for the prodigy. Often compared with Frank Rijkaard, he is also deified as a modern-time Franz Beckenbauer. In the local press he became the 'Kaiser d'Arkel'.

As a junior player it was already impossible to steal the ball from de Jong. At the time the size of a barely blooming tulip, he was sold to the academy of Ajax for . . . €1! His father, who was crazy about new-wave music and an absolute fan of the band Frankie Goes to Hollywood, named Frenkie after the group. In his bedroom little de Jong cut out posters and collected all Barça-related items. His role model was Sergio Busquets: he only had eyes for the great Catalan machine and spent time dissecting the slightest of his gestures.

Despite the fortune awaiting him at Barça and overwhelming popularity, 'FDJ', who partied in Amsterdam at the completion of an unforgettable cup championship double at the conclusion of his time in the Netherlands, promised to return to Arkel from time to time. It's good to remember your history, recharge your batteries and keep your feet on the ground.

DID YOU KNOW?

Before he had even donned the Barça jersey, Frenkie de Jong had made the sworn enemy – Real Madrid – cry. After an amazing victory by Ajax in March 2019 at Santiago Bernabéu, the Dutchman went to find his relatives in a hotel in Madrid. As related by the great Dutch daily *De Telegraaf*, he was welcomed by his family on his arrival and his parents quipped: 'Now you can really go to Barcelona!' No doubt the Camp Nou aficionados enjoyed that one!

DE JONG

Matthijs

DE LIGT

BORN: 12 August 1999
Leiderdorp,
The Netherlands

HEIGHT: 1.89 m

POSITION: Defender

PROFESSIONAL CAREER:
Jong Ajax, Ajax
Amsterdam, Juventus FC,
Bayern Munich

When you're aged 15 and you've already been named best player of tournaments reserved for the U-17s and then for the U-19s, there is obviously something special. It must be said, therefore, that the young Matthijs de Ligt enjoyed a rapid rise, imposing himself without any fear in the Ajax youth squad.

In September 2016 he started with the big boys, with a first match in the Eredivisie, the Dutch championship, against Willem II Tilburg, and he even scored a goal to celebrate his debut with Ajax, who triumphed 5–0. The new pearl from South Holland became, after Clarence Seedorf, the youngest scorer in the iconic Amsterdam jersey. It was a supersonic ascent for this incredible talent.

As a child and with racquet in hand he dreamed of following in the footsteps of Roger Federer or Rafael Nadal on the tennis courts, but it was football that claimed him. For this lifelong Ajax fan the first chills at the Johan Cruijff ArenA occurred when he was small. His father took him to follow his idols and he watched with stars in his eyes. He even posed for a photo with Luis Suárez, the ace goal grabber, on a match night when he was a ball boy.

At the school of the Lancers he surprised the coaches with his sense of investment in everything he did and his courage. Matthijs de Ligt never backed down, even when faced with opponents craftier than him. Did he develop this confidence when he, the big brother, defended his little brother Wouter and his twin sisters in the schoolyard?

In any case, the kid from FC Abcoude was still ahead of others. Full of confidence, the new captain imposed himself as a true leader in the midst of babies who would go on to charm Europe during the 2018–19 season. After overturning both Real Madrid and Juventus, Ajax just failed at the gates of the final against Tottenham Hotspur in the last four but won the double at home. Suddenly, the Lancers entered the hearts of the supporters.

It was no coincidence either that after their painful absences from Euro 2016 and the 2018 World Cup the Oranje armada was back in force, with Matthijs de Ligt as one of the most powerful and important representatives. It is now up to him to negotiate his transfer challenge to one of the biggest clubs in Europe after joining Bayern Munich. History is ready to be made.

DID YOU KNOW?

The 'little fat one' almost never set foot on the grounds of the Ajax training centre. At eight years of age the child was obviously a gifted football player – that's a fact – but the kid was also somewhat chubby. He was even nicknamed 'Bolle', Dutch for meatball or dumpling. Finally, after almost 12 months of hesitation, the green light was given for de Ligt to join the legendary Amsterdam club. 'When I landed there,' the blond colossus remembered, 'I was taken directly to a dietitian and placed on a diet!'

FRANCE

Ousmane

DEMBÉLÉ

BORN: 15 May 1997
Vernon, France

HEIGHT: 1.78 m

POSITION: Winger

PROFESSIONAL CAREER:
Stade Rennais FC,
Borussia Dortmund,
FC Barcelona,
Paris Saint-Germain FC

'I quit football!' It was through this shocking SMS in June 2015 that Ousmane Dembélé warned René Ruello, then president of Stade Rennes, of his dissatisfaction. Exasperated by the fact that his coach Philippe Montanier did not believe in him the young attacker, despite his youthful 18 years, showed a strong backbone.

Everything ended up going back to normal but, convinced of his own ability at the game, the gifted Norman, whose father is of Malian origin, and his mum, of Senegalese-Mauritanian origin, had to quickly learn the ropes. Capable of punching through any defence with his pace and footwork, Dembouz acquired this technique as a teenager when he flourished playing futsal.

At the age of 13 he was headed for Stade Rennais. His burst of speed, combined with his ease of bringing danger into opposition territory whenever he got possession of the ball, worked wonders. Good with both feet, the freakish ability to take on and more often than not beat his marker, leant some to accuse him of unnecessary dribbling and holding on to the ball too long. Shrugging off his critics, Dembélé approached life in Ligue 1 like an old veteran, accelerating his career to such an extent that he played barely 30 matches in the French top flight.

A transfer to Germany in the summer of 2016 followed, to the powerhouse of Borussia Dortmund, then coached by Thomas Tuchel, before an international debut for Les Bleus against the Cote d'Ivoire in a 0-0 draw in Lens. A fan of French cartoon *Olive and Tom*, Dembélé shows some of the characteristics of the duo, often employing sensational tricks and skills while playing the game with a smile on his face. His time in the Bundesliga showed his fierce work ethic as well, but the atmosphere became tense in the off-season.

Seduced by the prospect of a move to Spain and FC Barcelona, Ousmane came into conflict with the coaches of the Schwarzgelben who, understandably, were loath to lose one of their star prospects. Finally, Dembélé won his case and headed for Camp Nou.

Dembélé's Barca career was a frustrating one: despite brief glimpses of form and his undoubted class and ability, he was never able to settle at the Blaugrana. A switch to the bright lights of Paris, and PSG, will not lessen the limelight but might provide the home comforts he craves.

DEMBÉLÉ

DID YOU KNOW?

The current coach of Stade Rennais, Julien Stéphan, has long blooded Ousmane Dembélé in the Breton formation. The Rouge et Noir coach mastered his 'Dembouz' into a line-up that fulfilled his potential. 'It is more to his advantage if we play in a 4-3-3, because he is covered, he has less effort to make in recovery and thus repositions higher up the pitch. This allows him to express all his qualities in offensive transitions when space becomes available. There, he enjoys it!'

THE NETHERLANDS

Memphis

DEPAY

BORN: 13 February 1994
Moordrecht,
The Netherlands

HEIGHT: 1.78 m

POSITION: Forward

PROFESSIONAL CAREER:
PSV Eindhoven,
Manchester United FC,
Olympique Lyonnais,
FC Barcelona, Atlético
de Madrid

Much has been said about Memphis Depay and his character, but no one would deny that he is without charisma. Strong-willed, the Dutchman had a difficult childhood in which his father, of Ghanaian origin, often let him down – hence the desire for his jersey not displaying his surname. Extremely gifted when in possession of the ball, the tattooed speedster was earmarked for greatness at a very early stage but his meteoric rise to the top wasn't without its problems.

Memphis often exasperated his coaches with his haughty demeanour and perceived arrogance, even in the land where those attributes are often the hallmarks of great superstars. Confident of himself, the Dutchman arrived at Manchester United in the summer of 2015 wearing the club's famed number 7 on his back, a historic number that has previously been worn by giants of the game such as Cristiano Ronaldo, Eric Cantona and George Best. United legends all, this was a heavy legacy for a young man. He started off well at Old Trafford, his game lively and ethereal to begin with, but after a few months he ran out of steam. It was as though the promising trajectory of the Dutch phenomenon was visibly sagging under the weight of expectation.

Comparisons were something that Memphis Depay had to put up with throughout his early career. From his debut as a precocious 17 year old at PSV Eindhoven in 2011, he was quickly confronted by experts comparing him with players of a bygone era. Placed on the left wing, the Dutch striker quickly demonstrated his qualities: speed, excellent technique on both feet and a devilish ball strike, including on free kicks.

With José Mourinho arriving in the Mancunian changing room Memphis gradually began to be frozen out, losing his place in the team and sitting on the bench for large parts of the season. With this in mind, in January 2017 he took up the challenge in Ligue 1, signing for Olympique Lyon. Despite the initial doubts, the Lyon coach Bruno Génésio was enthusiastic about his new man. 'He is a hard-hitting, powerful player, capable of both creating and scoring goals,' the Gones coach commented.

Jean-Michel Aulas, owner of the club, predicted: 'Memphis will not be long in raising all in the stadium to [their] feet.' This was a premonition that duly materialised, albeit intermittently at first, but Memphis came good again and earned a transfer in 2021 to FC Barcelona. After two seasons at Barcelona Memphis switched allegiances, signing for La Liga rivals Atlético de Madrid.

Rúben

DIAS

BORN: 14 May 1997
Amadora, Portugal

HEIGHT: 1.86 m

POSITION: Defender

PROFESSIONAL CAREER:
SL Benfica,
Manchester City FC

Rúben Dias certainly knows how to make an impression at the highest level: a sensational performance against Paris Saint-Germain during the Champions League semi-final in 2021 is testament to that. In the first leg of that last-four encounter at the Parc des Princes and in tandem with John Stones, Dias was able to stifle the talents of Kylian Mbappé and company, a performance by the Portuguese defender that warmed the hearts of Citizens supporters.

Even if the epic run to the final ended in a feeling of unfinished business, City beaten in Dias's home country of Portugal when they lost the all-English showdown to Chelsea 0–1 in Porto, the stature and reputation of the committed centre back certainly grew. In a wink to fate, Dias grew up in Amadora only a stone's throw away from the Luz stadium, the mythical stadium of Benfica.

A nascent star in his youth from local side Estrela, Rúben joined the Eagles academy at the age of 11. With an old head on young shoulders he showed dazzling maturity for his age, and his coaches particularly appreciated his ability to stay focused for 90 minutes without relaxation. With a physique that belied his tender years, it was little surprise that he turned professional with the Lisbon giants as soon as he was eligible to sign.

Dias made his debut for Benfica in September 2017 against Rui Vitória in the domestic championship and his ascent was rapid. Later that year he rubbed shoulders with Marcus Rashford and Romelu Lukaku during a gala match against Manchester United. Despite the defeat against the Red Devils, 0–1, his immaculate performance did not go unnoticed. Unsurprisingly, the native of Amadora was swiftly on the radar of Portuguese coach Fernando Santos, Dias making the Portugal squad for the 2018 World Cup after excelling in the youth grades.

The former captain of the Portugal youth side didn't see a minute of playing time in Russia, but that did not dim his light. A year later, placed alongside José Fonte in the heart of the defence, Dias was a major part of the Nations Cup triumph against the Netherlands, Portugal winning 1–0. That was quickly followed in September 2020 by a thunderous announcement: Dias was off to the Premier League, Manchester City taking out the chequebook and investing €68 million to bring Dias to the north of England. At the end of his first season in England he was voted the best player by the local Manchester press. The only other Portuguese to win this award was Cristiano Ronaldo, twice: 2007 and 2008.

DIAS

DID YOU KNOW?

There was a funny welcome for Rúben Dias in October 2020 at Elland Road, the home stadium of Leeds United. Getting off the bus, the young Citizens defender was turned away by the security service because they had not recognised the Portuguese international. Before this Premier League match Dias had to wait for a member of staff to verify his identity before he could enter the changing room. Manchester City FC left Marcelo Bielsa's Leeds with a point in a 1–1 draw.

Luis

DÍAZ

BORN: 13 January 1997
Barrancas, Columbia

HEIGHT: 1.80 m

POSITION: Winger

PROFESSIONAL CAREER:
Barranquilla FC,
Atlético Junior, FC Porto,
Liverpool FC

A true revelation of the Champions League semi-final in Villarreal in May 2022, the Colombian winger playing for Liverpool was simply unstoppable: that evening in Spain he conquered everyone. Displaying his full range of dizzying tricks and skills on the left flank of the Reds attack, Díaz ran rings around the defenders of the 'Yellow Submarine'. After arriving at Liverpool just months earlier, Luis Fernando Díaz Marulanda burst into the hearts of fans of the English club.

With his incessant running, his terrific close control and dribbling skills and his enigmatic approach to taking on defenders, the former Barranquilla winger quickly became an adopted Scouser and had head coach Jürgen Klopp raving about his abilities. Díaz had landed in Liverpool in January 2022, signed from FC Porto, where he had spent just two and a half years following his rapid transition to European football, and penned a long-term contract with one of the giants of the game.

It was a great reward for Díaz, who is a big fan of Ronaldinho, and he was spotted in his country by a certain Carlos Valderrama. The former Colombian international and Montpellier legend spotted the budding Díaz in his homeland during a tournament that brought together amateurs, with the players all being from local ethnicities. The goal was to ascertain the best selection to compete in an indigenous version of the Copa América.

Luis Díaz comes from a Wayuu family, a Native American ethnic group that lives on the border with Venezuela. Some have rejected social contact. The future champion grew up in poverty, and to escape he needed to become a wizard with the ball at his feet. Little Díaz dared, tried and succeeded, with Valderrama taking him to Barranquilla FC. Nicknamed 'El Fideo' (the noodle) because of his slender appearance, the winger lit up the national stage with a range of superb matches.

In September 2018 he celebrated his first international selection for Colombia against Argentina in a 0–0 draw, and once in the team he didn't leave the group again. At the age of 21 he played in the final of the Copa Sudamericana with Atlético Junior, although they lost against the Brazilians from Club Athletico Paranaense. However, it wasn't a defeat that hindered his departure to Europe. Zenit Saint-Petersburg looked a likely destination but, on the advice of his compatriots James Rodriguez and Radamel Falcao, Luis Díaz finally opted for Porto. It was a wise choice that just a few months later opened the mythical doors of Anfield.

DÍAZ

DID YOU KNOW?

During the Copa América 2021 held in Brazil, Luis Díaz, with four goals, won the title of top scorer in the South American tournament alongside a renowned player – and not just any, since it was Lionel Messi! If the Argentine star ended up winning this 47th edition of the tournament, then the little Colombian was more than satisfied with the third step on the podium. During the classification match against Peru, which Los Cafeteros won 3–2, Díaz helped himself to a double.

ARGENTINA

Ángel
DI MARÍA

BORN: 14 February 1988
Rosario, Argentina

HEIGHT: 1.80 m

POSITION: Midfielder

PROFESSIONAL CAREER:
Rosario Central, SL Benfica,
Real Madrid,
Manchester United FC,
Paris Saint-Germain FC,
Juventus FC, SL Benfica

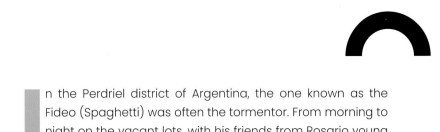

n the Perdriel district of Argentina, the one known as the Fideo (Spaghetti) was often the tormentor. From morning to night on the vacant lots, with his friends from Rosario young Ángel played with the ball, pretending to be his hero Diego Maradona. It lasted for hours and hours. In a quirk of potential destiny, little Di María was born not far from another future star of Argentine football, a certain Lionel Messi.

Twenty years later on the other side of the border, 'Angelito' was lighting up a remarkable World Cup in Brazil. His performances had the Albiceleste faithful fantasising about a third World Cup coronation, but catastrophe struck. The player who was making Argentina tick, the link between defence and attack, was injured in a clash against Belgium. He was a major doubt for the final at the Maracanã against Germany, and on the morning of the match Ángel begged coach Alejandro Sabella to let him play. 'If you put me on, I'll play until it blows!' Di María pleaded.

However, the Argentine boss did not want to take the risk, and Di María was forced to witness the game as a spectator, powerless in the stands while his team fell at the ultimate hurdle. Four years later and despite his desire for revenge, Angelito missed out again in the tournament held in Russia. He did score a spectacular goal against France, but the match in the round of 16 ended in a devastating 4–3 defeat. Redemption was finally his in 2022 in Qatar.

Seen as the ideal foil for Messi in the national team, Di María's rise to prominence wasn't as straightforward as it was for his prestigious former club mate. After making a name for himself in Portugal with Benfica, he experienced glorious success in La Liga with Real Madrid before a 2014 move to the Premier League with Manchester United. It was quickly evident that despite flashes of genius his style wasn't compatible with the Red Devils, and he struggled to acclimatise to the climate of northern England.

It was a Kafkaesque situation – and some assert that Di María is the perfect double of the Czech writer – and the move was ended and Di María made the switch to Paris and the stars of PSG. Even if his performances were intermittent, the Argentine number 11 appeared to rediscover his swagger. His tempo, technical ease and formidable precision in his long shot, especially on free kicks, dazzled. Di María only got the chance to show his qualities to the Turin faithful for one season before heading back to where it all began in Europe for the sprightly winger: SL Benfica in Portugal.

DID YOU KNOW?

With hands blackened by coal, the young Ángel went in the evening to training at Rosario Central. Barely a teenager, he hardly had time to change because during the day the son had to help his father to deliver coal to his customers. The Di María family was not a wealthy one but they were passionate about football. Ángel's father did not succeed in his attempt to shine in the River Plate jersey, and upon leaving the club he made the coal trade his profession.

ITALY

Gianluigi

DONNARUMMA

BORN: 25 February 1999
Castellammare di Stabia,
Italy

HEIGHT: 1.96 m

POSITION: Goalkeeper

PROFESSIONAL CAREER:
AC Milan,
Paris Saint-Germain FC

A teenager among the professionals! The first steps that Gianluigi Donnarumma made in taking his place between the posts for AC Milan perfectly illustrate an old coach's catchphrase: in the world of football, if you're good enough you're old enough. For the native of Castellammare di Stabia, a town located in the Gulf of Naples, life as a footballer was always at full speed ahead.

When Donnarumma joined the Napoli academy at the age of four, the kid who had gold between his hands was already dreaming of appearing in the famous red and black like his 'uncle' Ernesto, a fervent supporter of the Milanese club. It wasn't all plain sailing for the young stopper, as his incredible performances along with his huge frame – sometimes he was as much as 30 cm taller than his peers – led to suspicious looks from opponents each week. This obliged his mother Marinella to present his birth certificate every weekend to dispel any doubts as to his eligibility.

Very quickly the talent of the young goalkeeper crossed the borders of the Campania, spreading far and wide, with Juventus, Fiorentina, Roma and Udinese sending their scouts to try to secure the signature of the prodigy. However, 'Gigio' had already chosen his destination: AC Milan, where his brother Antonio, nine years his senior, was already evolving into a classy goalkeeper.

At Milanello the rise of the young hopeful, voted best goalkeeper of the European Under-18 Championship at just 17 years of age, was dazzling. Imperious in the air, endowed with excellent reflexes and solid on his line, it did not take long for Donnarumma to impose himself in the first-team goal, relegating the incumbent, Spaniard Diego López, to the substitutes bench when Donnarumma was just 16 years and 9 months old.

A cap for the national team soon followed. Giampiero Ventura, the Italian coach, called him up for a friendly match against France. Brought on in the second half, Donnarumma replaced his idol, the legend Gianluigi Buffon, and once again broke a record as a precocious youth. Regularly cited among the best goalkeepers of both Italy and Europe, the Italian had plenty of envious eyes cast his way. Milan did their best to extend his contract, but when it ran down in 2021 Gianluigi Donnarumma joined Paris Saint-Germain and brought strong competition to Keylor Navas. A heroic part in the penalty shoot-out win over England in the delayed Euro 2020 was the jewel in Donnarumma's crown.

DONNARUMMA

DID YOU KNOW?

His jersey number of a double 9 is not very common in the pantheon of goalkeepers, who are usually accustomed to a small number, but Donnarumma wears the number 99 simply in reference to his year of birth. He was born 25 February 1999 and became the second youngest goalkeeper to play in Serie A, ahead of monumental talents such as Gianluigi Buffon.

ARGENTINA

Paulo
DYBALA

BORN: 15 November 1993
Laguna Larga, Argentina

HEIGHT: 1.77 m

POSITION: Forward

PROFESSIONAL CAREER:
Instituto de Córdoba,
Palermo FC, Juventus FC,
AS Roma

DID YOU KNOW?

In Argentina, Paulo Dybala is nicknamed 'El Pibe de la pensión' (the kid of the pension) because, on the death of his father, the gifted niño with a ball at his feet was taken in by the centre of training at the Instituto Atlético Central Córdoba. In order to prevent him from having a gruelling travel schedule on a daily basis – from his home to the training grounds – the club preferred to grant the adolescent a boarder status. In August 2011, at 17 years of age, he became a professional player there.

O f Polish origin by his paternal grandfather and Italian by his maternal grandmother, Paulo Bruno Exequiel Dybala was born in the city of Córdoba in the north of Argentina. It was at one of the best training clubs in the city, the Instituto, where he scored his first goals and earned himself the nickname of 'la Joya' (the Jewel) by those who first witnessed the blossoming of his talent.

While still just a teenager Dybala began to beat all known youth records at the club: youngest goal scorer, youngest player to appear in the first team, first 17-year-old player to register two hat-tricks and score in six matches in a row!

A little over a year later he left Argentina, departing for the land of his ancestors and joining the squad of US Palermo in Sicily. Once again the South American broke records at a dizzying speed, including becoming the youngest player to score in the Palermo shirt. In three seasons he scored 21 goals in 93 games and made others sit up and take notice of this emerging talent.

The jump was immediate, and in the summer of 2015 Dybala was off, headed to northern Italy to join the prestigious ranks of the 'Old Lady', Juventus. Always searching for those rare gems, Juventus bet on Dybala to raise the spirits of a club that was going through a beleaguered period of existence. At the Bianconeri, midfielder Paul Pogba christened a new nickname for the prodigy. His French partner called him 'Carré R2', alluding to the keys used in some famous video games for performing a curling strike.

It wasn't long before Dybala found himself lining up alongside another idol: Lionel Messi, in the colours of the Argentina national team, came off the bench for the Albiceleste to replace Carlos Tevez in a FIFA World Cup qualifying match against Paraguay.

During the 2018–19 season the Argentinian Jewel lost some of his lustre and began a drought in front of goal. Perhaps the arrival of Cristiano Ronaldo into the black and white stripes changed his role and cost him a starting spot. For some Dybala might not be the player he once was, but talent is boundless and a switch to AS Roma and a new lease of life under enigmatic coach José Mourinho might be the prelude to a return to his dazzling best.

DYBALA

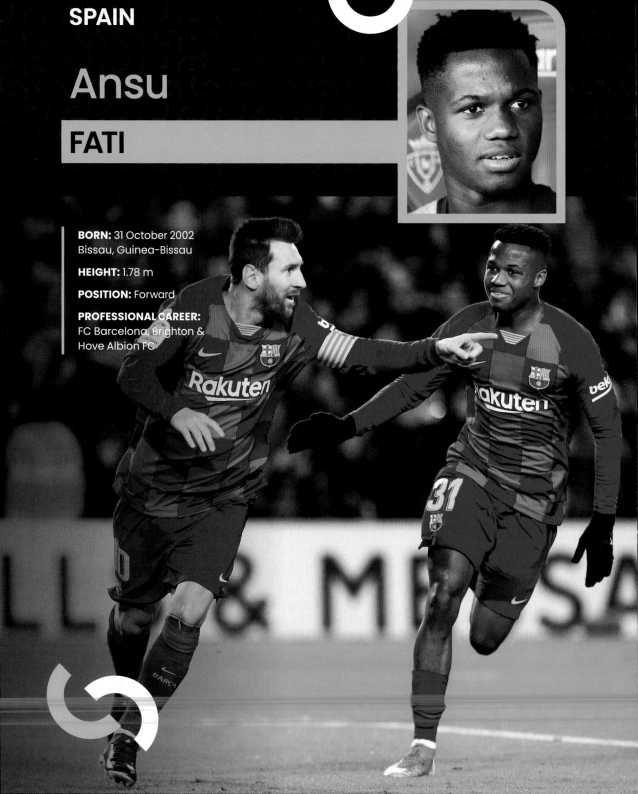

SPAIN

Ansu

FATI

BORN: 31 October 2002
Bissau, Guinea-Bissau

HEIGHT: 1.78 m

POSITION: Forward

PROFESSIONAL CAREER:
FC Barcelona, Brighton &
Hove Albion FC

'**W**e are potentially facing a footballer who can mark the beginning of a new era. The new Messi? These are big words, but can he be a world-class footballer? The answer is "Yes".' These aren't the opinions of just anyone but the thoughts of the midfield maestro Xavi himself when asked about the sheer quality of the young superstar that is Ansu Fati. When the old brain of Barça pronounces things this way it is rarely said lightly.

In truth, FC Barcelona is betting a lot on its favourite son, torn from the clutches of its hereditary enemy Real Madrid, who offered fabulous terms to Ansu's father Bori Fati, himself a former footballer. 'Real offered more money than Barça but we chose Barcelona, because the Catalan recruiters came to us with the contract and convinced me,' he revealed. Why did the Blaugrana put so much faith in this phenomenon? Well, because he is just that!

Anssumane Fati – his real name – has extraordinary passion and a real sense of purpose, although that often appears confusing to many who watch him. His style of play and laidback demeanour belie his aggressive will to win. Born in Guinea-Bissau, Ansu lived in Spain from the age of six. He first strapped on his boots at CDF Herrera, the Andalusian team of the area where his parents lived. A few months later Sevilla FC noticed his rare ability and flexibility and promptly signed him up. It didn't stop there, though, and before he was even 10 years old he arrived at La Masia, the famed Barcelona academy.

Despite a double tibia/fibula fracture at the beginning of his adolescence, the gifted Fati skipped through the age ranks at a rapid pace. In July 2019 Ansu Fati extended his contract with the Catalan club until 2022, with a release clause already set at €100 million! In the weeks that followed, even before his 17th birthday he beat a long-term youth record both in Spain and in the Champions League by making his Barcelona debut.

After struggling to cement a place in the Barcelona line-up, Fati made the switch to English Premier League outfit Brighton where, under Roberto De Zerbi, he has flourished in the top flight as well as impressing in the south coast club's maiden European campaign in the UEFA Europa League.

DID YOU KNOW?

Under Victor Valdés with the Juveniles Ansu Fati was more than pampered, but the former goalkeeper who became a coach remembered an incredible anecdote about the little wonder. 'During a tournament in Russia, he grimaced,' Valdes recalled. 'I told him to show me his boots, and their condition was disastrous. His pains came from there, so I bought him a new pair to make him feel better.'

PORTUGAL

João
FÉLIX

BORN: 10 November 1999
Viseu, Portugal

HEIGHT: 1.81 m

POSITION: Forward

PROFESSIONAL CAREER:
SL Benfica,
Atlético de Madrid,
Chelsea FC, FC Barcelona

A pinch of Rui Costa for his technical side, a hint of Youri Djorkaeff for his position in the team as a nine and a half, a good dose of Kaká for his offensive impact and some grains of Michel Platini for his vision of the game: here is the excellent recipe that fell in July 2019 into the melting pot of Atlético de Madrid. It was for this combination of promise and ability that the Colchoneros broke their piggy bank.

It was some bet to enlist a 19-year-old kid, certainly supremely gifted but still far from the finished article. João Félix himself was not about to get carried away and was keen to keep a low profile. 'I have understood that there were high expectations around me, but I never saw it as a bad thing. I still have been very calm in this phase of adaptation. I had the support of my family and friends, in addition to that of Atlético. The €126 million fee is never in my mind.'

It must be said that the little marvel has amazed at every stage, starting from when he burst onto the stage as a young talent. From his first steps his parents Carla and Carlos used to hide trinkets and precious objects in the living room, which the young scoundrel would hunt down. He discovered life-sized football at FC Porto at the age of eight; however, the Dragons in one of their less-inspired moves did not rate him, insisting he was too small and weak. Therefore, as a teenager he was allowed to leave for the enemy Benfica, the club rubbing their hands in glee at their acquisition.

In September 2016 João Félix became the youngest player to start with the Eagles Reserves, at the age of 16 years and 312 days. In April 2019, despite his braces recalling the precocity of his youth, he netted a sublime hat-trick, all registered with ease and relaxation, against Eintracht Frankfurt in the Europa League.

A counterattack specialist armed with an elegant dribbling ability, the little guy from Viseu lived two huge moments that summer: he conquered the maiden Nations League with Seleção das Quinas, Portugal claiming the title, before his record-breaking transfer to Atlético. A stint at Chelsea allowed Félix to show his skills in patches but intermittently so, with the Blues not taking the option to buy. Their hesitance allowed Barcelona to pounce, and the Portuguese schemer has the chance to shine at the Camp Nou and gain a new legion of supporters.

FÉLIX

DID YOU KNOW?

When he arrived at Atlético, João Félix wanted to wear the number 79 on his back; however, that request was denied because La Liga regulations require players to wear numbers between 1 and 25. Felix then attempted to claim the number 10 jersey but his wish was still not granted because Ángel Correa was assigned the lucky number. Finally, the young Portuguese received the number 7, which had been left vacant by Antoine Griezmann when he departed for Barcelona.

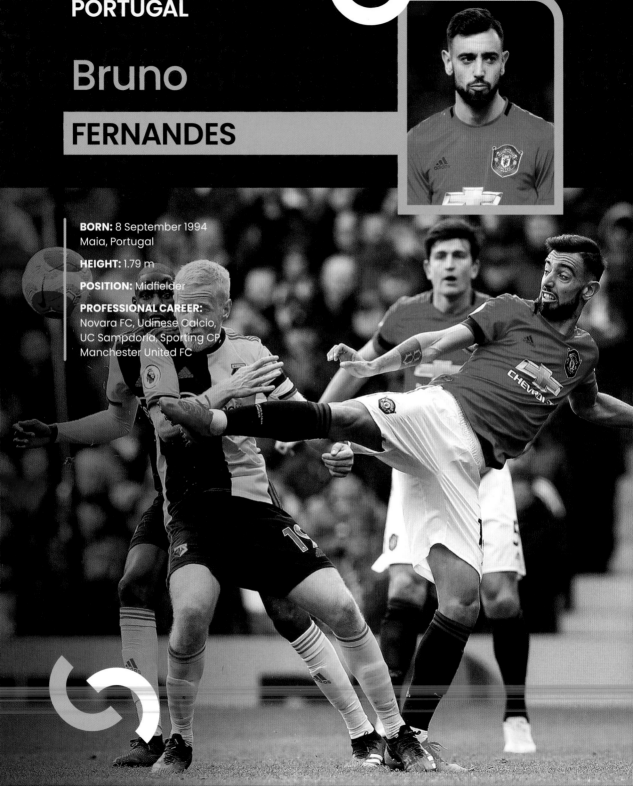

Bruno
FERNANDES

BORN: 8 September 1994
Maia, Portugal

HEIGHT: 1.79 m

POSITION: Midfielder

PROFESSIONAL CAREER:
Novara FC, Udinese Calcio,
UC Sampdoria, Sporting CP,
Manchester United FC

Be careful, as one Fernandes can hide another! On 10 November 2017 in Viseu in the 56th minute of a friendly between Portugal and Saudi Arabia, which the hosts won 1–0, Manuel Fernandes gave way to a newcomer Bruno Fernandes. It was a big step for the former student of Boavista, his trajectory seemingly ever on an upward curve.

To complete his training the 'Canon de Maia' (Maya's canon) – his nickname in his hometown – set sail at the age of 17 for Piedmont. He earned his junior stripes on the green grass of Novara Calcio, between Turin and Milan, not the normal hunting ground for a Portuguese youth. With his natural class and in a country marked by exceptional champions, the kid was quickly decked out with the nickname of 'little Maradona'.

Everything was moving at a rapid rate for Bruno but he was able to stand tall, showcasing his ability to always be well placed, have an eye for a pass and, despite his young age, have the lucidity without rushing to find the best path to goal for himself or for others. Despite this silk Fernandes still embraced steel, a style he was ready to assume for the good of the team.

'I am certainly a player who sacrifices themselves,' he said. 'Sometimes I know I exaggerate my actions on the field and give in to the pressure of the moment, but it's because I want to occupy every part of the field and be involved everywhere.' Fernandes discovered a high level of football in Serie B, but it was at Udinese that he first encountered the true elite of Italian football.

After five years of apprenticeship in Italy, enhanced by a season at Sampdoria on loan, Bruno Fernandes returned home and signed for Sporting. In Lisbon the public discovered yet another nugget of Lusitanian football. Technically sound, Fernandes had no problem in standing out, distinguishing himself in terms of assists in the Portuguese League. On the wish list of Real Madrid, the young attacking midfielder ultimately opted for the British Empire. In January 2020 for €55 million, Bruno Miguel Borges Fernandes found himself donning the famous red shirt of global behemoth Manchester United.

A five and a half year contract saw Fernandes become the sixth Portuguese player to put on the mythical Manchester United jersey. A thundering debut season was followed by goals and assists aplenty as Bruno racked up a swathe of personal awards at Old Trafford, quickly cementing himself as the heartbeat of the team and a firm fan favourite.

DID YOU KNOW?

In March 2020 during the derby against Manchester City, Bruno Fernandes crossed swords with Pep Guardiola. Both men got confused to say the least. On a throw-in the Catalan manager pretended to give him the ball back before throwing it to Luke Shaw instead. An exchange of words followed between the two protagonists before the Portuguese invited Guardiola to be silent by pointing his index finger to his mouth. United had the last laugh: they won 2–0.

Enzo
FERNÁNDEZ

BORN: 17 January 2001
San Martin, Argentina

HEIGHT: 1.78 m

POSITION: Midfielder

PROFESSIONAL CAREER:
CA River Plate,
Defensa y Justicia,
Benfica, Chelsea FC

At every World Cup there's a breakout star, and in Qatar in late 2022 it was undoubtedly Enzo Fernández. The Argentine midfielder came from nowhere to win the FIFA Young Player Award following his country's triumph on football's biggest stage.

The dynamic midfielder collected his prize following, arguably, the greatest World Cup final of them all. As the post-game scene unfolded, Fernández could be forgiven for having a look of disbelief in his eyes: the 21-year-old's story is among the most remarkable in recent times. Remarkable, as Fernández only made his senior international debut in September 2022, coming on as a second-half substitute in a 3–0 friendly win over Honduras. The occasion saw Fernández fulfil a lifelong ambition to play alongside his idol, Lionel Messi.

Fernández secured his place in the squad following mature displays in two pre-tournament friendlies and having continued to excel for Portuguese club side Benfica. His rare combination of energy, perfect technique and tactical intelligence saw him swiftly acclimatise to European football following his move from boyhood club River Plate. He was a key figure for a Benfica side that swept all before them at home and abroad. The team remained unbeaten across 28 matches in all competitions and finished top of a UEFA Champions League group featuring Messi's Paris Saint-Germain.

The youngster's passing is crisp, incisive and precise, with an accuracy rate of 90 per cent in league matches in 2022 and 88 per cent during the World Cup. His ball-striking ability was memorably displayed in Argentina's do-or-die group-stage win over Mexico, when he expertly curled a shot into the top corner of Guillermo Ochoa's net to seal a 2–0 victory. He had come on as a substitute in that game but thereafter started every remaining match of Argentina's triumphant World Cup campaign.

Fernández was at his best in the showpiece final as Argentina overwhelmed France in the opening 70 minutes of the contest. Kylian Mbappé turned the game on its head as the match developed into an all-time classic, but Fernández's Argentina dug deep to eventually triumph in the most dramatic circumstances.

Having played just six months for Benfica, he was purchased by English Premier League club Chelsea in January 2023 for a British-record transfer fee.

DID YOU KNOW?

In 2016 Enzo Fernández posted an open letter on Facebook to his future teammate Lionel Messi, urging his hero to reconsider retirement from international football. 'Please don't go, Leo,' he wrote. 'Seeing you play with the light blue and white is the greatest pride in the world.' Thankfully, for Enzo and for everyone else, Messi did just that and went on to win the greatest prize of all in 2022.

Roberto

FIRMINO

BORN: 2 October 1991
Maceió, Brazil

HEIGHT: 1.81 m

POSITION: Midfielder

PROFESSIONAL CAREER:
Figueirense FC,
TSG Hoffenheim,
Liverpool FC,
Al-Ahli Saudi FC

There was always talk around Roberto Firmino. As early as 2009 and just after celebrating his 17th birthday the Brazilian star spent a month with fabled club Olympique de Marseille. Despite impressing to a degree, the attacker was not taken on by the giants of southern France. 'He was offered to us, then we took him to trial with the reserves,' Jean-Philippe Durand, one of the recruitment managers at Marseille, recalled. 'He was very skilful in front of goal and was technically very good. However, he was a kid who had just come from his country; he was a bit lost.'

That was bad luck for Marseille. In December 2010 German club Hoffenheim took the gamble on recruiting the South American. After scoring 49 goals in 153 games across the Rhine, it proved to be a gamble that paid off. A move to the Premier League in June 2015, signing for Liverpool for €40 million, pitted Firmino in a front three alongside Sadio Mané and Mohamed Salah, the triumvirate affectionately known as 'MSF'. This trident led Liverpool to glory.

Along with his game intelligence, the Brazilian also illustrated his desire to win. More in the shadows than his two attacking partners, 'Bobby', as the fans on the Red side of the Mersey liked to call him, sacrificed himself in an often-thankless role. Roberto Firmino was happy to play the pivoting role up front, making runs away from goal to free up space for those positioned in the wider roles.

With this relative sacrifice, the native of the state of Alagoas scored fewer goals than his accomplices. That's hardly a blight on a player who knows where the net is and has often scored vital goals at crucial times. Besides, since the arrival of Jürgen Klopp on the Reds bench in 2015 the German technician has insisted that the Brazilian play more advanced and take more risks, such as the day in December 2018 when, author of a hat-trick, he steamrolled the Arsenal defence in a crushing 5–1 win.

A more discreet performance but nonetheless critical came when Liverpool won the ultimate crown, the UEFA Champions League in 2019, Firmino playing well in the 2–0 win over Tottenham Hotspur. After eight seasons lighting up the field in the Reds, Roberto switched to Al-Ahli in the Saudi Pro League at the commencement of the 2023–24 campaign.

ENGLAND

Phil

FODEN

BORN: 28 May 2000
Stockport, England

HEIGHT: 1.71 m

POSITION: Midfielder

PROFESSIONAL CAREER:
Manchester City FC

'My dad is obsessed with red, while Mum is more into sky blue,' Phil Foden said of his familial ties to Manchester's big two. Indeed, his dad is a supporter of United while his mum swears only to the Citizens. It was a tug of war that was won by Mum, little Phil preferring to follow matches at the City of Manchester Stadium, the home of City. Sitting with eyes wide open and watching on as players such as Joey Barton barked out instructions to his teammates had an effect on the young boy.

At the age of seven Foden made his first strides in the game at Reddish Vulcans, a modest Stockport club recognised for its qualities in the training of young talent. This was where Foden played his adolescent football before joining Manchester City. Joe Makin, the scout who saw his talent and recommended him to City, remembers the way Foden stood out: 'He was the shortest on the pitch,' he said, 'but you gave him the ball and all that took a back seat.'

As a ball boy at City Phil Foden scrutinised his idols of the time: James Milner, Adam Johnson, Gareth Barry and Owen Hargreaves. Foden was also passionate about the dexterous technique of a Samir Nasri or a David Silva. At the end of one match Sergio Agüero patted him on the head. Little did Phil know that four years later the Argentine international known as 'Kun' would become his teammate.

Director of football at the Citizens, the Spanish technician Txiki Begiristain encouraged Pep Guardiola to observe the phenomenon. Guardiola agreed right away that Foden was the real deal, and suddenly Foden became one of his favourite players. 'It's a gift for us and a diamond for England,' the Catalan coach raved. A rarity as an Englishman winning a starting place in the cosmopolitan make-up of the City squad, the young winger impressed with the variety of his game and his ability to read the play and create danger for opponents from all over the field.

Complemented by the quality of Kevin De Bruyne, Riyad Mahrez and latterly Erling Braut Haaland, Phil Foden has few equals. 'Every time he doesn't play I apologise to him,' Guardiola confessed as he worried about the future of his jewel, who was impatient to gain a regular spot in the star-studded City team. 'He is the only player who cannot be sold, under any circumstance. Not even for €500 million.' It appears there is no limit to what Foden is worth to his hometown team.

DID YOU KNOW?

In December 2017 there was an appearance record for Phil Foden who, against the Ukrainians of Shakhtar Donetsk, became the youngest English player to start in a Champions League game. The previous month, at 17 years and 177 days of age, he had become the fourth youngest English player to play a European match when he replaced Yaya Touré against Feyenoord Rotterdam.

SPAIN

GAVI

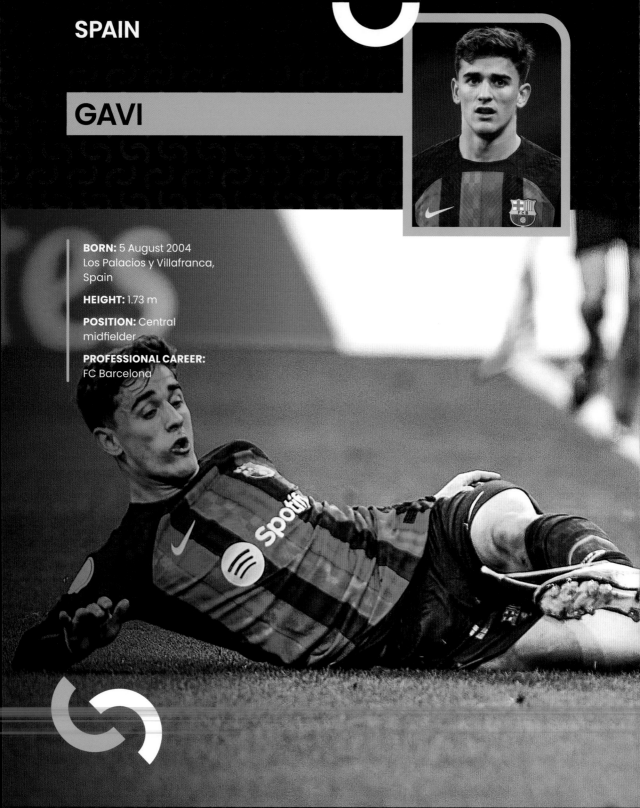

BORN: 5 August 2004
Los Palacios y Villafranca,
Spain

HEIGHT: 1.73 m

POSITION: Central
midfielder

PROFESSIONAL CAREER:
FC Barcelona

ere is the latest little genius of Spanish football. Pablo Martín Páez Gavira, better known by the nickname 'Gavi', is the new hope of La Roja, absent of such a flamboyant player since the retirement of Andrés Iniesta in the Selección midfield. At the age of 19, this is a player at ease in each of his gestures and never panicked thanks to his technical quality. The indolent Andalusian burns with pace, skill and creativity.

With incredible lucidity in his risk-taking, a disconcerting calmness on the ball and a volume of stunning games already dispatched to the archive, the darling of the Camp Nou impresses with every match played. He had only six La Liga fixtures under his belt with Barça before Luis Enrique in the fall of 2021 began calling on him to participate in the final four of the Nations League in Italy. Even more incredible is that Gavi did not even go through the usual route of youth ranks, playing barely any U-18 matches and none for the U-20.

In Milan, Italy was unable to resist the Spanish charge, Spain winning 2–1 in the semi-finals. Only France, thanks to a goal from the legendary striker Karim Benzema, were able to douse the Gavi flame. Six months later against the Czech Republic he became, at 17 years and 304 days of age, the youngest scorer in the history of the Spanish national team. The boy didn't make any noise about his personal feats, though, preferring to let his natural ability with the ball at his feet do the talking for him.

Faced with his obsession with football, dad Pablo registered Gavi at Betis Seville, close to his family, so he could satisfy his passion. In a single season Gavi scored 95 goals in the youth team, displaying his unbelievable ability at any early age. The talent of the young Andalusian quickly went beyond the borders of the south of the Iberian Peninsula. Real and Barça were already following this unique case, but it was the Catalan club that attracted the gifted eleven year old, who was invited to join the academy at La Masia, the Blaugrana training centre.

Shortly before turning 17 Gavi joined the professional team, then he was launched into the senior arena by the-then manager of Barça, Ronald Koeman. At only 18 years and 156 days, after the Basque Iker Muniain (Athletic Bilbao), Gavi became the second youngest player to reach the mark of 50 matches in La Liga. That was quicker than Leo Messi, Fernando Torres and his teammate Ansu Fati! Spanish football is reassured: without a doubt the country has her new jewel.

DID YOU KNOW?

Gavi has seen some things in his career, but he was surprised by something picked up by a young strategist. Alert to the smallest detail, an FC Barcelona coach has still not come back from it: 'Gavi has the bad habit of playing without lacing his boots!' the coach revealed. 'One day, as a joke, I asked him to show me if he knew how to tie them. He replied to me that he had not been able to do so. I told him, "One day your opponents will step on you, or you will fall!" He told me he felt more comfortable like that . . . I didn't want to upset him. Otherwise, he would no longer be Gavi!'

GAVI

Olivier

GIROUD

BORN: 30 September 1986
Chambéry, France

HEIGHT: 1.93 m

POSITION: Striker

PROFESSIONAL CAREER:
Grenoble Foot 38,
Istres, Tours FC,
Montpellier HSC,
Arsenal FC, Chelsea FC,
AC Milan

He is both the second-best scorer in the history of Les Bleus and the striker who became world champion in Russia without finding the net once. That's the whole paradox of Olivier Giroud, essential to the national team but a player who has never had the unanimous backing of either coaches or fans. Criticising Giroud is even a national sport, so much so that on the eve of France versus Australia, the first match of the World Cup in Russia in 2018, there were not many people who protested his absence from the starting XI. At the end of the game the same observers who claimed his head were clamouring to see him back, because in a sluggish attack against the Socceroos the combined efforts of those selected ahead of him just weren't good enough.

Today, Giroud is an attacker who has proved his worth in some of the biggest clubs in Europe. By no means a goal-scoring machine, he is always there to create openings for others and will often find the net himself in big matches. A presence in the national team for a long time, Giroud was seen as indispensable in the eyes of Didier Deschamps. 'It's when he is not there that one realises all the importance that he has for the team,' the French coach commented.

This strong relationship was briefly undermined with the return to favour of Karim Benzema in the blue shirt and the rise and rise of Kylian Mbappé. In all the clubs he goes to, Giroud scores. While he might be less prolific than some strikers, he did finish as top scorer in the Europa League the year Chelsea won the title. Devastating in the final against his former club Arsenal, he was involved in three goals and left the Gunners regretting his release.

Upon his arrival in Italy with AC Milan he was instrumental in helping them to their 19th scudetto. His career choices allowed him to settle into the national side for a period longer than most expectations. A member of an exclusive club of players with more than 100 appearances in the national team, he overtook Thierry Henry to become France's all-time leading scorer when he netted against Poland at the 2022 World Cup in Qatar and can rightly sit alongside the greatest French internationals of all time.

Giroud is arguably one of the eternally most misunderstood and underrated forwards in the game, partly because he doesn't have the profile of the modern striker or the ability to dribble or sprint past opponents. However, he has made history, and that is something reserved for only legends of the game.

GIROUD

GERMANY

Serge
GNABRY

BORN: 14 July 1995
Stuttgart, Germany

HEIGHT: 1.76 m

POSITION: Midfielder

PROFESSIONAL CAREER:
VfB Stuttgart, Arsenal FC,
West Bromwich Albion FC,
Werder Bremen,
TSG Hoffenheim,
Bayern Munich

It's a good idea not to annoy Serge Gnabry. During his time with Arsenal in the Premier League the talented player didn't have it all his own way and often struggled to cement a place in the Gunners starting line-up, but no matter: Serge would have his revenge, and in some style. In an unforgettable return to London in the colours of German champions Bayern Munich, Gnabry put Tottenham Hotspur to the sword, scoring four times in an incredible 7–2 victory against the team that had played the final the year before.

To register a quadruple in the Champions League is not for everyone, but to back it up a few months later with another superlative display – this time against Chelsea – was a new punishment that the English fans were not able to digest. This wasn't the Gnabry whom Chelsea had seen in the past; was it really the same player? The Gnabry that the Blues crossed paths with earlier hadn't been as mature, or as decisive or as strong.

Arriving at Arsenal as a callow youth of 16, Gnabry was introduced to the London public as the Gunners third-youngest player in Premier League history, behind only Jack Wilshere and Cesc Fàbregas. He didn't play as often in the early days, unable to make much of an impression in nine matches. An unconvincing loan at West Bromwich Albion sent him back to square one, and uncertain of his future. Even worse, he appeared to have lost the backing of manager Arsène Wenger.

The numbers didn't argue in favour of Gnabry. With the Gunners since 2012, he played only 18 games for one goal. It was clearly time for a move back to where he came from, not in his native town of Stuttgart but in a club in search of its glorious past: Werder Bremen. It was a marriage of convenience that turned into passion and allowed the career of the young German to take off.

He impressed the Bundesliga and the watching world, earning a move to Bayern Munich for €8 million and establishing himself there, ensuring life after Franck Ribéry and Arjen Robben seemed secure in Allianz Arena. A switch appeared to have been flicked and suddenly Gnabry clicked, sparking into life. At the age of 25 he had by far the best season of his career, and it's not just on the club stage that he shone.

As part of a new wind of change blowing through Die Mannschaft, Gnabry struck a memorable hat-trick on his international debut. He was the first German to achieve the feat since Dieter Muller had done so in 1976.

GNABRY

DID YOU KNOW?

Gnabry celebrates his goals by making the gesture of turning a teaspoon in a cup. After intriguing fans of the Bundesliga, he revealed his source of inspiration. 'I am a big fan of the NBA, and especially of James Harden,' he revealed. 'The Houston Rockets point guard celebrates his decisive baskets in the money time with this small gesture, "stir the pot", which means "What's in my cup is really hot!" Like me on the field.'

Jack
GREALISH

BORN: 10 September 1995
Birmingham, England

HEIGHT: 1.75 m

POSITION: Midfielder

PROFESSIONAL CAREER:
Notts County FC,
Aston Villa FC,
Manchester City FC

Throughout his teenage years Jack Peter Grealish sang the anthem of his country of origin – Ireland – the land of his ancestors, and he proudly wore the green jersey, but in September 2015 the Birmingham phenomenon finally chose to put on the white shirt of the Three Lions.

At the age of six he joined the academy of Aston Villa, his local club and one that has a storied history. It was a baptism of fire, a welcome to the world of football as Grealish looked to circumvent the physical challenges that inevitably came the way of the fleet-footed playmaker.

Endowed with a special technique, little Jack showed the heart of a champion. He was influenced by his Celtic heritage and played Gaelic football alongside his football training. At 16 years of age he was promoted to the Villains professional group; however, faced with severe competition, Grealish accepted a loan move to Notts County, then in League One. It wasn't long before he grabbed his first goal, in December 2013 when he dribbled past three Gillingham defenders to find the net.

A versatile player, this creator and king of improvisation can also serve as a torchbearer and provide leadership from any position across the front line, and with each touch he can dictate the tempo of the match. He has been likened to former England international Chris Waddle. A year after his maiden goal his big day came, a Premier League debut for Aston Villa, who were lined up against Manchester City. In May 2015 he progressed further, appearing for Villa in the FA Cup final, a first appearance at Wembley Stadium that ended in disappointment when Arsenal won 4–0.

Having had a taste, Grealish became more focused and celebrated a first Premier League goal in a 5–1 hammering of Norwich City in October 2019. Less than a year later, in September 2020, he made his England international debut in a 0–0 draw with Denmark. He played in the Euro 2020 final against Italy and shortly afterwards transferred to Manchester City for what was a Premier League record deal of €117 million. The fee summed up the incredible rise of the young Brummie star.

DID YOU KNOW?

You had better believe that the highest level in football is in the genes of the family of Jack Grealish: his great-great-grandfather Billy Garraty, an honourable Aston Villa striker, won the FA Cup ... in 1905! That day, at the Crystal Palace stadium in front of more than 100,000 supporters, the flagship club of Birmingham defeated Newcastle United 2–0. And that's where his grandfather received the famous trophy.

FRANCE

Antoine

GRIEZMANN

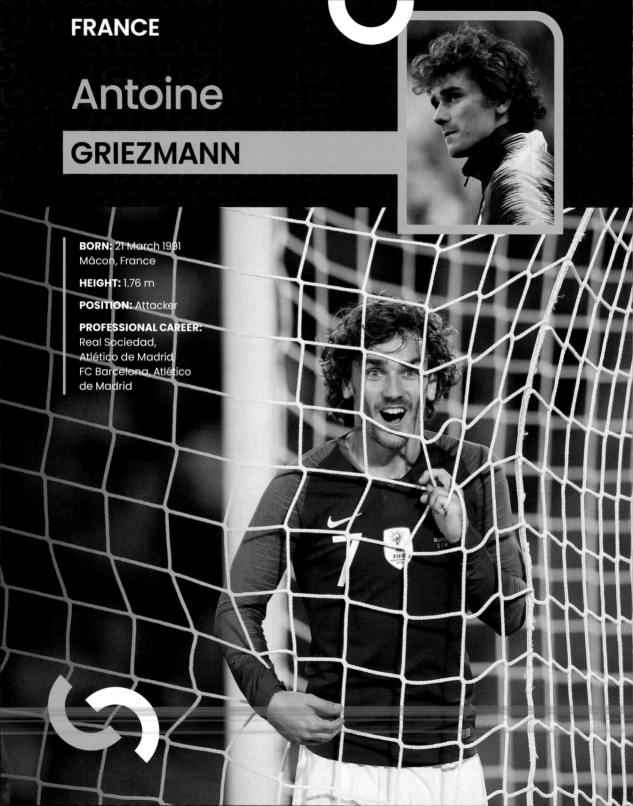

BORN: 21 March 1991
Mâcon, France

HEIGHT: 1.76 m

POSITION: Attacker

PROFESSIONAL CAREER:
Real Sociedad,
Atlético de Madrid,
FC Barcelona, Atlético
de Madrid

DID YOU KNOW?

Yet another proof of the flaws in the French training system, Antoine Griezmann fell through the cracks as a child. Although tested almost everywhere in France he never convinced, and this for one reason: his size. The main regret in the Griezmann camp was FC Metz, whose coaches had promised him a contract then retracted. 'We are not going to take your son because he is too small,' they finally admitted to Antoine's dad. Big mistake . . .

Is Antoine Griezmann really French? On his ID it's clear – 'Born in Mâcon on 21 March 1991 – yet this exciting talent is a pure product of Spanish football. He failed to be spotted by clubs in his homeland, and it was in exile from the age of 13 in San Sebastian in Basque country that he was spotted by renowned talent scout Éric Olhats. Olhats became a kind of surrogate father, and under him Griezmann flourished.

Real Sociedad appreciated his technical quality, which had been rejected by a French system that was fond of big guys. Griezmann never played a single minute in a match in Ligue 1; his playground was La Liga. Forced to take his talent to a country that values the technical player, he worked on the full range of his repertoire in Pays Basque.

He began to make a name for himself under the tutelage of Philippe Montanier at Real Sociedad and exploded as a world star under the thumb of Diego Simeone at Atlético de Madrid. France did see glimpses of him, of course, during a representative career at youth level that took in France U-19s, U-20s and U-21s.

Back home the adopted Spaniard continued to pile up the goals, and in March 2014 Didier Deschamps couldn't ignore him anymore. He summoned Griezmann to the big boys and offered him his first international selection against the Netherlands. Two months later Griezmann's name was no longer a surprise when it was included in the list of 23 who would fly to Brazil for what would be Antoine's first World Cup.

In South America Antoine Griezmann began his love affair with the national team, coming to the fore under a coach who was only too happy to give him the keys to the attack. In tears following the elimination in the quarter finals against Germany, two years later he became the top scorer of Euro 2016 with six goals. That wasn't enough to pick up the title, though: France was beaten by Portugal in the final at the Stade de France.

However, 'Grizi' once again got back among the goals and in 2018 he triumphed in the Europa League, scoring a double in the final against Olympique de Marseille. Two months later he lifted the World Cup in Russia as part of a dominant French team. That year he arguably deserved the Golden Ball, but Croatian Luka Modrić was the one who was acknowledged as the king. A stint at Barcelona followed before a return to Casa Simeon and Atlético. He must have missed the Madrid air!

GERMANY

İlkay

GÜNDOĞAN

BORN: 24 October 1990
Gelsenkirchen, Germany

HEIGHT: 180 m

POSITION: Midfielder

PROFESSIONAL CAREER:
FC Nürnberg,
Borussia Dortmund,
Manchester City FC,
FC Barcelona

The spine is vital, and especially for an athlete at the highest level. İlkay Gündoğan learned this the hard way in the autumn of 2012. During an international break, he landed badly and spent a night in hell; a subsequent MRI revealed a root infection in the nerves in his vertebrae. This was a hammer blow for this piston of the midfield who, at only 22 years of age, suffered atrociously.

To everyone's surprise he left for treatment in the Crimea, near Ukraine. 'My volleyball player cousin suffered from the same injury. She was well cared for there,' was the justification of the German international of Turkish origin. Coming from Gelsenkirchen in the middle of the Ruhr, he logically performed his first steps on the grass at Schalke 04, the big local club. As a teenager he joined his half-brother Paul Johar at VfL Bochum to complete his training.

By then İlkay had earned a reputation as a playmaker across the Rhine. An innately talented one, he created opportunities and distributed wonderfully, a purveyor of sumptuous passing benefiting from a panoramic view and a unique sense of tempo. In short, he was the hub of his team. Some considered him slow at this stage, but his massive importance to the team meant that his coach at Borussia Dortmund, Jürgen Klopp, considered him vital and hatched a plan to get the best from his technician.

Klopp slowed the tempo of the performance a notch and made Gündoğan a relay in the centre of the park, a position for which he is now renowned. In the latter months of 2011 Joachim Löw in turn cracked the code and selected Gündoğan within the Nationalmannschaft for the first time.

After five seasons on the banks of the Rhine, in June 2016 Gündoğan opted for Manchester City FC. It was a good deal for the Sky Blues and for Pep Guardiola, who enlisted one of the best specialists of his position on the continent for only €25 million. 'He is so smart that he understands the game perfectly,' Guardiola insisted. 'He knows in every action what is the best for the group.' Installed at the Citizens, the cerebral German has a bright future ahead of him if his back leaves him in peace. All good things come to an end, though, and Gündoğan's love affair with City ended at the start of 2023–24 when he left to join Barcelona. He departed with some present: two goals in an FA Cup final victory over rivals Manchester United, securing part two of Manchester City's treble.

DID YOU KNOW?

The thunderbolt triggered in May 2021 by the giants of European football, all eager to create a Super League, was little denounced by its main actors. The footballers were discreet – except İlkay Gündoğan, one of the few to speak about this project. 'Some always want more matches. Anyone thinking of us players?' he asked. 'The current Champions League format works very well and that's why it's popular.'

NORWAY

Erling Braut

HAALAND

BORN: 21 July 2000
Leeds, England

HEIGHT: 1.94 m

POSITION: Striker

PROFESSIONAL CAREER:
Bryne FK, Molde FK,
FC Red Bull Salzbourg,
Borussia Dortmund,
Manchester City FC

Faced with the infernal growth curve of the young man the medical staff from Molde, the Norwegian club where Erling Braut Haaland played, put him on enforced rest. The future star was then only 17 years old but already had tremendous potential. All the more atypical was that the chubby-faced Viking grew up in the United Kingdom, where his father, Alf-Inge Haaland, was a professional footballer from Nottingham Forest to Manchester City via Leeds United, where the future sharpshooter had been born.

On the pitch the young starlet began playing with adults from the age of 15, lining up for Bryne FK during a modest cup match in Norway. He had a trial in Germany at Hoffenheim, but the leaders of the Baden-Württemberg side denied him a contract because the demands of one were outside their usual pay scale. Thus Haaland started in the professional ranks on 1 February 2017 with Molde, his protective club that was then being trained by Ole Gunnar Solskjær, the future Manchester United manager. In August 2018 he was recruited by Red Bull Salzburg, but he did not land in Austria until six months later. That was the beginning of the explosion of this prodigy.

Everything really clicked when the season resumed in the autumn of 2019. Under the prism of the Champions League the public discovered the Norwegian machine whose quickdraw shooting, pace and silky touch were allied with an impressive physique that dominated defenders. In half a dozen Champions League group matches Haaland slammed in eight goals, including a hat-trick in his first match against KRC Genk that was won 6–2. He also found the net against Liverpool and Napoli.

In the Austrian championship the Norwegian Gulliver scored more goals (29) than he had played matches (27). In December 2019 Borussia Dortmund took a chance on the phenomenon, and in his first game in the Bundesliga on 18 January 2020 he began to repay them. Brought on in the 56th minute as the Schwarzgelben trailed FC Augsburg 1–3, a 26-minute hat-trick gave Dortmund a remarkable 5–3 win.

A City fan since early childhood, the new Sky Blues striker joined Guardiola at the club in 2022 and hit the ground running amid a blaze of goals and a swathe of hat-tricks. The Norwegian hitman broke record after record in his Premier League debut season, scoring 52 goals as Manchester City claimed the treble of Premier League, FA Cup and the Holy Grail of the UEFA Champions League.

DID YOU KNOW?

A fervent practitioner of meditation, Erling Braut Haaland regularly indulges in yoga. It is from this discipline that he draws his celebration when he scores: he sits, legs crossed and hands open, in the posture called siddhasana. During the U-20 World Cup in May 2019 he might well have abused this use after plundering nine goals against Honduras, with the young Norwegians recording an astonishing 12–0 victory.

MOROCCO

Achraf

HAKIMI

BORN: 4 November 1998
Madrid, Spain

HEIGHT: 1.81 m

POSITION: Defender

PROFESSIONAL CAREER:
Real Madrid,
Borussia Dortmund,
Inter Milan,
Paris Saint-Germain FC

Being trained at Real Madrid is not a guarantee for a place under the sun. The Merengues club stacks the ranks with stars and imports far more players than they tend to promote through the youth ranks. Achraf Hakimi started his journey from slightly further afar: born in Morocco, he moved to Getafe in the Madrid suburbs when his parents took the family from North Africa to Spain. His undoubted talent saw the door of the Real Madrid training institute open to him at just seven years of age.

Hakimi's model was a hairy Brazilian with a Portuguese accent and fantastic runs up and down the left channel. He had Marcelo as his idol early on and dreamed of the day he might evolve enough to play alongside him. Shy and persevering, the Moroccan believed in his lucky star and refused to go and see if the grass was greener elsewhere. If it was going to be hard to break through well, so be it.

He hoped to catch the eye of head coach Zinedine Zidane, who was never afraid to take a look into the Madrid nursery and see what rough demands could be taken and polished. Hakimi lacked neither guts nor talent. He quickened the pace of his acceleration as he was eager to progress alongside his training partners, who were all patiently waiting for their turn to shine. Climbing the ladder at a rapid rate, the Hispano-Moroccan found himself doing summer preparations with the professionals even though he was not then old enough to drive a car.

With pace and technique Hakimi's attacking style seduced Zidane, and the Madridista coach did not hesitate to call him for training with Ronaldo and gang before throwing him into the deep end at 19 years of age. A plethora of injuries to those in front of him saw Hakimi burst from almost complete anonymity to holder of the right-back position. In the process he became the first Moroccan to wear the Real Madrid shirt in an official match, then he scored his first professional goal on the Bernabéu pitch after a strike was created by Karim Benzema.

He became the first Atlas Lion to lift the big-eared cup as Real conquered Europe again. However, the fall was to be brutal. Zidane's surprise departure from Real did not help Achraf, and his status as a regular starter did little to resist the return of the Madrid wounded. Borussia Dortmund sniffed an opportunity and took the player on loan before he was transferred to Inter Milan, then he made a move to France with Paris Saint-Germain in 2021.

DID YOU KNOW?

When Real Madrid was looking for a way out for its young player in 2018, Olympique de Marseille (OM) inquired about Hakimi's availability. The sports director at the time, Andoni Zubizarreta, led the first approach but the proposed deal was quickly abandoned. Achraf was perceived to be too young and not physical enough for Ligue 1. Finally, he joined Dortmund in the Bundesliga as one of the best in the world at his job and is now out of the price range for OM. It is their rival, PSG, who have him on the roster.

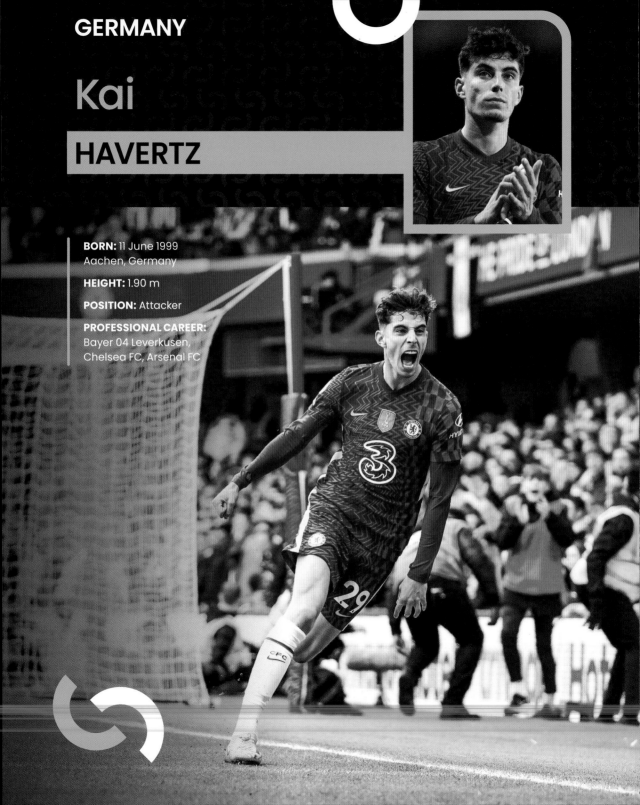

GERMANY

Kai

HAVERTZ

BORN: 11 June 1999
Aachen, Germany

HEIGHT: 1.90 m

POSITION: Attacker

PROFESSIONAL CAREER:
Bayer 04 Leverkusen,
Chelsea FC, Arsenal FC

I n the midst of a health and financial crisis, most of the leaders of European football thought twice before splurging in the transfer market – but there is always an exception to the rule. The club that did the breaking was Chelsea, and the person involved was Kai Havertz. The Blues did not dither in their pursuit of the promising German, who had already been making waves in his homeland. The youngest player to pull on the shirt of Bayer 04 Leverkusen in the Bundesliga, at the age of 17 and 126 days, his performances quickly earned admirers from beyond the German borders.

Tall, technical and with excellent vision, Havertz can do it all. The price of the phenomenon raised eyebrows, Chelsea happily paying the €80 million requested by Bayer Leverkusen for this 21-year-old international. Whether this would prove valuable – well, the future soon told us it would.

The stage was the Estádio do Dragão in Porto in the final of the 2021 Champions League. At the tail end of the first half Havertz was played in by Mason Mount and, faced with Ederson advancing in the Manchester City goal, did not hesitate, slipping the ball into the net for what was to be the match-winning goal. It had taken some time for Havertz to register his first goal, but he instantly became the unexpected hero of the Blues as Chelsea won the European Cup for only the second time in their history.

It was a spectacular happy ending in what had been a particularly difficult season for Kai Havertz. Taxed as the most expensive player of the summer transfer window in 2020 the expectation was enormous, and each appearance was closely scrutinised. Indeed, he was persistently reminded of his transfer fee throughout the season, something the German shrugged off. 'Obviously it's a big transfer, but I think it's normal in football at the present time to spend such sums,' Havertz said. 'So, it does not put me under too much pressure, because I don't play well or badly because of the price of my transfer.'

The arrival of compatriot Thomas Tuchel on the manager's bench to replace Frank Lampard kick-started Havertz's campaign. Like the whole team, Havertz metamorphosed and gradually returned to the starting XI before scoring the famous goal in the final against City as a regular. 'Havertz has qualities,' Tuchel commented. 'He needs to show them. It's that simple!' Havertz ruffled a few feathers in London by switching blue for red in 2023–24, taking his considerable talents from West to North London by signing for Arsenal.

HAVERTZ

DID YOU KNOW?

If it was with his grandfather Richard that Kai touched his first footballs, it was with his big brother that he got a taste of music. Guitar for the eldest, Kai played his first notes on his grandmother's piano and caught the music virus. He continues in his free time to play his favourite melodies, as it is a way to decompress and avoid false notes in his career.

ENGLAND

Jordan
HENDERSON

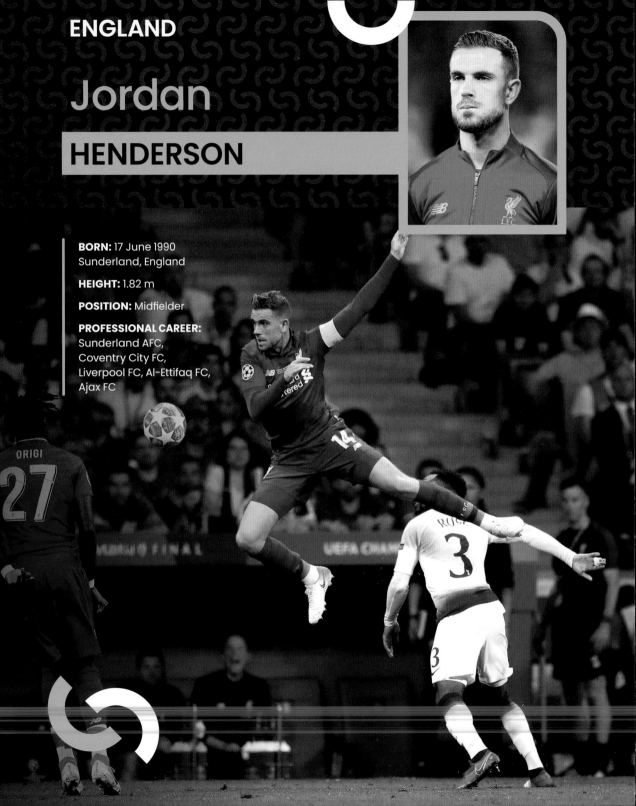

BORN: 17 June 1990
Sunderland, England

HEIGHT: 1.82 m

POSITION: Midfielder

PROFESSIONAL CAREER:
Sunderland AFC,
Coventry City FC,
Liverpool FC, Al-Ettifaq FC,
Ajax FC

I n mechanics a cog shines less than a cylinder, but without this essential piece of the engine it's impossible to start! In football it is the same thing. At the heart of the red machine, playing his part to the full, leading his team to the title and as celebrated as he should be, Jordan Henderson shines.

The Reds' general in chief is not a pretender to the golden ball, but 'Captain' Henderson is at the head of an exceptional troupe, a team that was crowned as the best in Europe in 2019 after their UEFA Champions League triumph over Tottenham Hotspur. Both for his club and when he is selected for England he always puts in a solid performance that is universally acknowledged. After years of questioning he has found a state of grace.

Henderson is unanimous in his position. The wearer of the captain's armband at Liverpool may not be the best midfielder in England by the numbers: better players who might show more than Henderson offensively or defensively can always be found, but how many midfielders can claim to be classified among the best in different categories? Henderson is part of this unique group.

His leadership, tactical role and impact in duels shatter the work of game analysts. The influence of the tall blond with the square jaw escapes standard formats and cannot be measured by statistics alone. He is an archetypal midfield general, a player who goes into battle with his eyes closed and a player who is the perfect voice to provide information from his coach.

So the wind turned. Gone are the days of timid beginnings with Sunderland and on the greasy pitches of Coventry City, where Henderson cut his teeth on loan in order to learn his trade and get important minutes under his belt. The Roman soldier-like fighter became a centurion: he was a unifying, respected personality and was recognised as such by his peers.

Better yet, the former Black Cat triumphed where the city kid Steven Gerrard, the Liverpool legend, tripped. Henderson brought back to the banks of the Mersey a trophy that had eluded the Reds for 30 years. Henderson brought his Liverpool tenure to somewhat of a surprise conclusion at the commencement of the 2023–24 season, shifting to the burgeoning Saudi Pro League and signing for Al-Ettifaq, a shift not without its controversies that led to an earlier than expected departure to Ajax in the Netherlands.

DID YOU KNOW?

Minutes after lifting the big-eared Champions League cup, the captain of the Reds cracked in the arms of his father. At the edge of the pitch, father and son remained entwined for long seconds, bursting into tears in the middle of the accredited photographers. Suffering from throat cancer in 2013, Jordan's father refused to see his son during his chemotherapy but attended the European coronation of his offspring in Madrid – to the sound of the famous song 'You'll Never Walk Alone'. Few would argue that this was the most emotional scene of the match.

HENDERSON

FRANCE

Lucas
HERNANDEZ

BORN: 14 February 1996
Marseille, France

HEIGHT: 1.84 m

POSITION: Defender

PROFESSIONAL CAREER:
Atlético de Madrid,
Bayern Munich

I t is the surprise guest who does not skimp on small gifts that are most welcomed and adopted by their hosts. Three months away from the 2018 World Cup in Russia, with Benjamin Mendy having been freshly operated on and the cruciate ligament of his right knee requiring treatment, talk involved who would replace him on Les Bleus left flank. The names Layvin Kurzawa, Lucas Digne and Jordan Amavi were mentioned, each having their backers.

Someone who wasn't in the conversation was Lucas Hernandez. His entry into the squad, at the Stade De France in a 2–3 loss to Colombia in March 2018, allowed the young man from Madrid to show his potential to the French public. 'Loukass' really had nothing to lose in selection and, without pressure, he blended into the tricolour group and seduced his coach.

Didier Deschamps had persuaded him a few weeks earlier to join the France group, but above all urged him not to follow up on his wishes to respond to the invitation of the Iberian Federation.

'When I say that Spain gave me everything, personally and professionally, it is a truth,' the native of Marseilles insisted. 'I spent my entire football career there until then. Not excluding the fact that I speak better Spanish, but that does not prevent my country from being France!' Capped, the adopted Castilian didn't leave the line-up, and from his sensational debut he scaled the heights. His country landed the supreme title in Moscow in only his 12th international match!

Hernandez is a relentless trainer: Deschamps was just one coach who appreciated his intense approach to sessions. The left side of Atlético has a vice that is appreciated by the boss of the Blues and by his deputy, Guy Stéphan. With such a pit bull in the ranks, defensive guarantees are assured.

Trained and forged in the hard school of the Colchoneros, Lucas Hernandez demonstrated mental and tactical discipline that was well above average at a young age. When selecting their best XI from those who played in La Liga, the experts were almost unanimous in picking Hernandez for the left-sided defensive berth, and in the summer of 2019 when he arrived at Bayern Munich it was with the strong esteem of the German public. With such qualities, Loukass seems to have signed a long lease not just with France but with the perennial Bavarian champions as well.

DID YOU KNOW?

Lucas Hernandez's brother Théo was, like him, born in Marseille and trained at Atlético. Loaned to Real Sociedad in 2018, the cadet also evolved to the left-side position. A former defender at Toulouse and Sochaux-Montbéliard and then at Marseille, their father, Jean-François Hernandez, also played in La Liga for Compostela, Rayo Vallecano and Atlético between 1998 and 2002. In the grip of serious financial difficulties, the father fled Spain in 2004 without leaving an address and all trace of him was lost in Thailand.

Theo
HERNANDEZ

BORN: 6 October 1997
Marseille, France

HEIGHT: 1.84 m

POSITION: Defender

PROFESSIONAL CAREER:
Atlético de Madrid,
Alavés, Real Madrid,
Real Sociedad, AC Milan

One Hernandez can hide another! Do you know Lucas? Then you will love Theo: the same aggressiveness, the same thirst for victory and the same blue jersey with the rooster on the chest. Theo Hernandez walks in the footsteps of his older brother, and it's not uncommon for the French national team defence to be 50 per cent populated by the same family. Nothing seems to resist the young talent; you only need to ask the supporters of the Rossoneri to understand the esteem in which the AC Milan left back is held.

Indisputable and essential alongside the likes of Zlatan Ibrahimović and the local Italian stars, Theo's cannon shots and defensive nous allowed the former club of Silvio Berlusconi to regain its lost glory. Theo takes on all obstacles and everything that revolves around them and more often than not comes out on top. Currently, everything is going pretty well for him. It is often when he is on vacation in Spain that the career of the youngest Hernandez does go awry.

The first time was in June 2017 on the Costa del Sol in Marbella. Theo was enjoying the sun and the beaches at the Rally of Hopes rather than attending France U-21 training under Sylvain Ripoll. 'I did a mistake of youth,' Hernandez said. 'I will also say that I was not pushed to go, which some people may have hoped, but that I chose Spain. There was my transfer to Real Madrid, which I was negotiating at that time. That, more that, more that . . . But I made an error.'

Theo admitted the stupidity of his act and was quickly forgiven, and the second time was a little more glorious. The scene took place in the heat of Ibiza at an appointment with a legend, Paolo Maldini, the current technical director of Milan. It changed everything, albeit in a good way this time. Everything was accelerating, and Théo signed for the Italians and soon settled as a starter in the Milan rearguard.

Beyond his achievements, which a good accountant would struggle to keep tally of, his pace, technique and athletic qualities make him an essential cog of Stefano Pioli's XI. His ability to run all day, both in defensive coverage and on offensive surges and especially in the last minutes of matches, impressed everyone. Of course, this praise has been rained freely on the native of Marseille, who had made a place for himself in Serie A. It was an express adaptation that could not leave anyone indifferent, including Didier Deschamps.

DID YOU KNOW?

The presentation to the public is a moment known to impress the eyes of the club's fans, but it can also prove embarrassing if the technique is not there. Ex-Real Madrid left back Theo Hernandez made it a bitter experience: officially presented at the Santiago Bernabéu stadium, the young Frenchman indulged in the traditional photo session in front of the press before doing some juggling but, alas, it didn't go as planned. Theo was embarrassed to manage just six juggles, a failure that fortunately was without consequences for the future.

Ciro

IMMOBILE

BORN: 20 February 1990
Torre Annunziata, Italy

HEIGHT: 1.85 m

POSITION: Forward

PROFESSIONAL CAREER:
Juventus FC, Robur Siena,
US Grosseto,
Delfino Pescara,
Genoa CFC, Torino FC,
Borussia Dortmund,
Sevilla FC, Torino FC,
 SS Lazio

On 27 July 2016, when he feverishly signed his contract in favour of Lazio, Ciro Immobile realised his dream: to sign with a club that lived up to ambitions that would bring him fulfilment and glory. Immobile, the little supporter of the club of his region of origin Napoli, experienced a chaotic early career.

Seven seasons tossed between disappointed hopes at Juventus, where he began the training and tests at Genoa and Torino from which he was not invited back. Not to mention those unlikely loans and two painful experiences abroad. The dyed in the wool Neapolitan notably judged his time at Borussia Dortmund as a monumental failure: 'When you don't speak the language, then you are not integrated into the team,' he said. 'It is difficult to adapt to a new country and a new championship.'

With no main interested party marked by his aborted adventure in the Bundesliga, Immobile's confidence was dented to the point of doubting his ability to become a professional goal hunter. As for his loan to Sevilla FC, it was not that confusion and misunderstandings with his teammates were the issue but more problems with his coach at the time, a certain Unai Emery. Before Ciro lost his market value his agent, Monchi, decided to set in motion a move away from Spain as soon as possible.

Above all, it was Lazio that provided refuge for him. It was a return to the fold armed with a fierce will to take, finally, his revenge on fate. The Italian striker was a recovering cause, and he worked like crazy at the Biancocelesti and quickly became the darling of the Lazio tifosi, which gave him wings and made him quite simply unplayable.

During the 2019–20 season he broke the record as the fastest Lazio player to reach the 100-goal mark and began to be mentioned as the potential top striker for the Italian national team. The Neapolitan caused consternation, though, as Italy preferred a 4–3–3 and not the 3–5–2 to which he had become accustomed at club level. This caused Roberto Mancini to hesitate between Andrea Belotti and him.

This debate will rage for quite some time as the two attackers vie for the starting place, even if Immobile leads with the beneficence of the majority of pundits. His thirst for victory works in his favour. Eventually made captain of Lazio, Ciro was crowned Champion of Europe with Italy when they defeated England at Wembley Stadium in the Euro 2020 final.

IMMOBILE

In the summer of 2018 while on vacation with his family on a beach in Abruzzo, Ciro Immobile was accosted by a man armed with a knife. However, the player already had his suspicions about the robber and he and his relatives turned away the attacker, who fled and was eventually arrested by the carabinieri. It was later learned this disreputable character was a fan of Lazio's rival club Pescara.

BRAZIL

Gabriel
JESUS

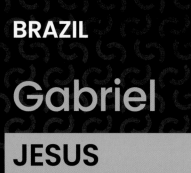

BORN: 3 April 1997
São Paulo, Brazil

HEIGHT: 1.75 m

POSITION: Forward

PROFESSIONAL CAREER:
SE Palmeiras,
Manchester City FC,
Arsenal FC

No one had imagined such a trajectory for a kid who grew up in a derelict district in the north of the megalopolis of São Paulo, more precisely in Jardim Peri. The young Brazilian had to fight to stand out from the very beginning. Raised with his three brothers by his widowed mother, little Gabriel Fernando de Jesus suffered from the absence of a father. On the pitch and despite his precocious ease with the ball, he passed through the football mesh unnoticed.

The teenager was even playing in defence when he put on the green and white jersey of the modest Pequeninos do Meio Ambiente. At the age of 15, when future professionals are already on the circuit being groomed for stardom, Gabriel evolved with the Associação Atlética Anhanguera and was noticed by a Palmeiras scout. A conclusive test soon followed when he donned the famous jersey of the great Paulista club, created more than a century ago by Italian migrants.

'Like everyone, I was first struck by its speed,' Bruno Petri, his trainer at the club, recalled. 'Above all, he had one more thing: he was determined.' Gabriel was aware that he had fallen behind others, so he worked harder. In Brazil he was called a 'white fly', a player who has had an atypical career. As if by chance, upon his induction into the cutting edge of the first team Palmeiras won the national title that had eluded them for 22 years. With 12 goals in 27 matches and voted best player in the Brazilian championship, Gabriel became the hero of the green people.

In a few months he put aside all the shortcomings in his game: his tactics, heading game and deficiencies were a thing of the past. Even the elders at Palmeiras were impressed by the little genius, and they weren't the only ones. Manchester United, Barcelona, Real Madrid, Bayern Munich and Paris Saint-Germain were all on the hunt for the Paulista pearl.

However, a phone call to the player from Pep Guardiola in the summer of 2016 made the difference. While Gabriel led the Seleção to the Olympic title during the Rio Olympics, he agreed to join Manchester City. Doubts were quickly swept away, and despite some physical hiccups the young Brazilian exploded in dynamite mode with the Citizens then continued on in that same vein upon transferring to north London giants Arsenal.

JESUS

PORTUGAL

Diogo

JOTA

BORN: 4 December 1996
Porto, Portugal

HEIGHT: 1.78 m

POSITION: Midfielder

PROFESSIONAL CAREER:
Paços de Ferreira,
Atlético de Madrid,
FC Porto, Wolverhampton
Wanderers, Liverpool FC

H is legs begin to wobble. On 14 November 2019 in the last minutes of a European Championship qualifier between Portugal and Lithuania in Faro, there was reason to tremble. As the defending champions romped to a 6–0 victory the 84th minute saw a debut for a novice, Diego Jota, who was replacing the master Cristiano Ronaldo, who had just completed a hat-trick. Inside the head of the gifted young talent doubts jostled: he was replacing the man for whom he had great admiration. He was replacing 'CR7'.

What an incredible rise for the young man of Porto who had stayed the course. At the age of 17 he signed with the prestigious Atlético de Madrid, for whom he would never play! Tossed from loan to loan, Diogo José Teixeira da Silva – his real and full name – finally set fire with the Dragons of Porto before traveling to England. The arrival on the Wolves bench of his compatriot Nuno Espírito Santo helped to facilitate the move.

The Lusitanian armada of Rui Patrício, João Moutinho and Rúben Neves in the Wolves squad helped to assist the integration of the promising winger. It took him but a short time to start piling on the exploits at Molineux, the Wolves' iconic home venue. When he moved to the Premier League in 2018 Jota, after 13 matches without scoring a single goal, finally found his groove: in January he scored a hat-trick against Leicester City and became the first Wolves player to achieve this in the top echelon since John Richards had done so 42 years earlier!

Jota's performances helped this great club from just outside Birmingham to return to continental action for the first time since 1980, with the Wolves qualifying for the Europa League. Inevitably, with a strongly atypical profile and such versatility – even if he still had to show consistency – Diogo Jota was suddenly on the radar of the best clubs. Because he is not a physical monster, the young Portuguese relies on superb vision and devastating pace.

It was Liverpool who seized the jewel in September 2020, and competition from the Firmino-Mané-Salah trio didn't put him off the switch. Between injuries and the COVID-19 crisis the Reds' bench was empty, and Jota proved his worth. Jürgen Klopp even screamed that his impact substitute was a genius. The German coach was under the charm of Jota, just like the Anfield fans, who compared the small-of-stature forward to star striker of the 1990s Robbie Fowler.

JOTA

DID YOU KNOW?

Diogo Jota truly entered the Liverpool Football Club record books by scoring the 10,000th goal in Reds' history. The event occurred on 27 October 2020 during a Champions League match against the Danes of Midtjylland that Liverpool won 2–0. A beautiful moment was achieved 128 years after the very first goal scored by a certain Jock Smith in 1892 against Higher Walton, a game the Reds won 8–0. It was also the 370th goal Liverpool had scored in the most prestigious continental competition since their debut in 1964.

BRAZIL

Vinícius

JÚNIOR

BORN: 12 July 2000
Sao Goncalo, Brazil

HEIGHT: 1.76 m

POSITION: Winger

PROFESSIONAL CAREER:
Flamengo, Real Madrid

Just crowned world champion for the second time in his career, Ronaldo (the real one!) arrived in Madrid, where Florentino Pérez did not hesitate to drop €45 million to ease him from the grasp of Inter Milan. Nearly 16 years later it was in the guise of the godfather that Ronaldo trod the lush green grass of the Santiago-Bernabéu Stadium again, this time to accompany 18-year-old Vinícius Júnior, who had arrived from Brazilian side Flamengo.

The Brazilian left winger may have cost the same sum as his companion – €45 million – but the spectators did not rush to attend his little session of juggling that day. However, with his label as the seventh-most expensive player in the history of the Merengues and the second-most expensive La Liga transfer in the summer of 2018, behind Thomas Lemar at Atlético,

Vinícius Júnior could expect the red carpet to be rolled out for him. But, no! Adored at the Maracanã Stadium in Rio in the jersey of Flamengo, he found himself playing matches with Castilla. The Spanish third division was a baptism of fire in European football, and daily life was not as glamorous as he imagined it would be when he left Rio de Janeiro. 'Vini Jr', though, proved himself with Castilla and ended up sitting on the bench facing Getafe to get a closer look at the band of Benzema.

Appearances were fleeting, but the Brazilian winger did not get impatient and decided not to use a clause in his contract that would have allowed him to return on loan from January 2019 to Flamengo if his position on the bench continued. A move back then might have signalled the end of his dream with the Merengues, especially since a certain Rodrygo Goes, a 17-year-old left winger nicknamed the 'new Neymar', was supposed to arrive from Santos, from where he was bought for, ironically, €45 million.

Time was running out for Vinícius Júnior, but he seized his chance when it was given to him and put in some formidable performances. However, an injury slowed his progress. Victim of a rupture of the tibia-fibula joint in the right ankle in a Champions League match against Ajax Amsterdam, he came back faster than expected in training but was ultimately not selected for the Copa América alongside his great idol Neymar. They have already rubbed shoulders within the Brazilian national selection; how long before they are reunited at club level?

DID YOU KNOW?

In Vinícius Júnior's case Manchester United had a head start on the transfer of the Brazilian nugget, but the South American did not immediately tread the grass of the Theatre of Dreams. This was the fault of the chief executive of United, Ed Woodward, who procrastinated over the deal. Discussions dragged on and allowed Barcelona and Real Madrid to enter the race for his signature. In the end, Madrid won the day.

JÚNIOR

ENGLAND

Harry

KANE

BORN: 28 July 1993
Walthamstow, England

HEIGHT: 1.88 m

POSITION: Striker

PROFESSIONAL CAREER:
Tottenham Hotspur FC,
Leyton Orient, Millwall FC,
Norwich City,
Leicester City FC,
Tottenham Hotspur FC,
Bayern Munich

Harry Kane has been central to England's trophy hunt since 2015, first captaining his national side two years later. His 2018 form saw him finish that year's World Cup as the tournament's top scorer, finding the back of the net six times in Russia. He then became the UEFA's top scorer in both the 2020 European and 2022 World Cup qualifiers, scoring 12 goals in each. His performances during Euro 2020, which included four goals, saw him lead England to their first major final since 1966.

This cursory glance at Kane's recent successes makes it hard to believe there was a time with the Three Lions when the striker struggled with his form. Arguably, being Wayne Rooney's successor was never going to be an easy task. Prior to being named England's 119th captain in 2017 Kane had encountered a 12-month goal drought. You can only be impressed by the mental strength and fortitude it took for him to turn struggle into success.

This was not new to Kane, though. Nicknamed 'Hurrykane' by English supporters due to his exploits at Wembley, the striker had started his career as the butt of their jokes. During his adolescence, everything from his accent to his physicality drew criticism. Encumbered by his height, the young player appeared too slow, too scrawny and lacking in tactical ability. To put it bluntly, his ability to ever be able to compete in the Premier League was questioned.

Sceptical coaches at Tottenham's football academy repeatedly sent out the young Kane on loan, hoping the discreet and ungainly teenager could progress. Starting out at Brisbane Road with League One's Leyton Orient, he then ventured to The Den to play for cut-throat Championship side Millwall FC. This was followed by spells at Norwich and Leicester City, each step seeing the Londoner gain in skill and confidence as he put his body on the line in front of hostile crowds.

Years later Kane spoke of the impact of his time on loan, specifically with Millwall. 'I was 18, we were in a relegation battle and it turned me into a man. I played in difficult, high-pressure games and I managed to come out of it positively.'

The summer of 2023 saw Kane at the centre of a transfer saga that captivated the world. Having given Tottenham Hotspur his all, breaking the club goal-scoring record, Kane was a wanted man. Eventually, it was German giants Bayern Munich who snagged the number 9, the Bavarians reaping the rewards of a sensational start to life in Germany for England's skipper, who began his German career in a blizzard of goals.

KANE

DID YOU KNOW?

The Tottenham hero previously wore the kit of Spurs's sworn enemy, Arsenal FC. Harry Kane played for the North London rival's club academy in 2001–02 as an eight year old, having joined them from his local side Ridgeway Rovers. His time with the Gunners was short lived, with Arsenal releasing him after a year. He went on to sign with Tottenham in 2004, the club he supported as a child.

FRANCE

N'Golo

KANTÉ

BORN: 29 March 1991
Paris, France

HEIGHT: 1.68 m

POSITION: Midfielder

PROFESSIONAL CAREER:
US Boulogne CO,
Stade Malherbe Caen,
Leicester City FC,
Chelsea FC, Al-Ittihad

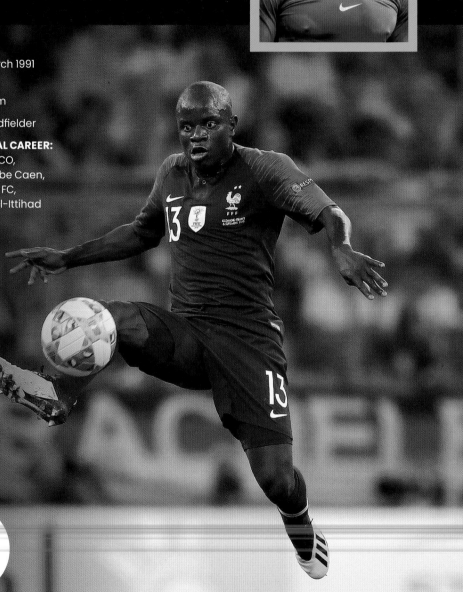

French head coach Didier Deschamps was bitterly disappointed upon hearing the news that his midfield talisman would miss the 2022 FIFA World Cup due to injury. A mainstay in France's starting line-up for half a decade, the diminutive player's absence was a blow to Les Bleus because N'Golo Kanté is a paradox, being unavoidable and indefensible on the field while remaining completely modest and shy off it. As a man he garners respect; as a player he shines. His work rate, defensive plays, attacking creativity and tactical knowhow always betters the team as a collective. Said simply, he is an overall top bloke and good teammate.

From a young age Kanté often played up age levels. While most predicted a career as a professional, he originally struggled to find a place at a football academy: 'too small' was a comment often used by scouts and recruiters. It wasn't until the age of 21, when he played for French Ligue 2 side Boulogne-sur-Mer, that his exploits started to draw attention. He then moved to fellow Ligue 2 side Caen, where his game went to another level.

He participated in the promotion of his new side to Ligue 1, where he joined the elite of French football. This introduction quickly made him the revelation of the 2014–15 season and led to his multi-million euro recruitment by Leicester City. His first season in England became a fairytale, his new English club stunning the football world by winning the Premier League – in part due to Kanté's contribution. Creative, fast and dynamic, N'Golo dazzled. 'One day, I'm going to see him cross the ball, and then finish the cross with a header himself,' his head coach, Claudio Ranieri, stated.

Chelsea FC bought Kanté at the end of the season and won the Premier League a year later. Former England international and pundit Gary Lineker tweeted: 'Leicester with Kanté: Champions. Without Kanté: struggling. Chelsea last season: struggled. With Kanté: top. Coincidence? I don't think so.'

Kanté won the PFA Players' Player of the Year. His individual and collective achievements continued with Chelsea, from two FIFA FIFPro World 11 appearances to the UEFA Europa League and Champions League and the highest prize: the World Cup. There is one thing that Kanté has not shied away from and that is winning trophies, which he aims to continue at new employees Al-Ittihad in the Saudi Pro League.

DID YOU KNOW?

Born in Paris to Malian parents, N'Golo Kanté could have played for the Mali Eagles. However, he ended up representing France, making his debut in 2016 against the Netherlands. Two years later he was a World Cup champion.

KANTÉ

Joshua
KIMMICH

BORN: 8 February 1995
Rottweil, Germany

HEIGHT: 1.76 m

POSITION: Midfielder

PROFESSIONAL CAREER:
VfB Stuttgart, RB Leipzig,
Bayern Munich

If you were asked to nominate a German footballer with stereotypical metronome qualities you need not look further than Joshua Kimmich. The Bayern man has evolved into a perfect balance between attack and defence and is one of the best number 6s around. With his tactical intelligence, versatility in the middle of the pitch and utility as a right back during Pep Guardiola's stint with the Bavarian side, Kimmich has long been the beating midfield heart of both Munich and Germany's squads. Confident and strong, 'Jo' is known for his mental resilience and capacity to motivate the sides he plays in, with style to match.

This style can be traced to Rottweil, between the Black Forest and bourgeois Stuttgart and Kimmich's parents' garden, to be precise. The problem, though, was young Jo's destruction of his parents' backyard while bouncing the football off a wall. A move to the local amateur football club, and an instruction to play at the end of the laneway if itching for a kick with his friends at home, started a journey that led to the game's highest levels.

Kimmich trained first with Bösingen. He then moved to the Bundesliga side of VfB Stuttgart's academy. The teenager continued to develop there and slowly built his skills, but he never signed with the top-flight German side. One of his coaches even told the youngster, 'You are not good enough, your body is not strong enough.' It was with third-division side RB Leipzig that Jo signed in the summer of 2013.

He moved to Bundesliga giants Bayern Munich ahead of the 2015–16 season and never looked back. Consistent performances during his first season combined with a double trophy win – the DFB-Pokal and Bundesliga – saw the young player called up to the national team's 2016 European campaign in France. The following year he became the Mannschaft's youngest captain.

After Germany's disastrous exit at the 2022 FIFA Men's World Cup, when Kimmich said he was afraid he'd fall into a hole few doubted his resolve to drag his national side to the pinnacle of international football.

DID YOU KNOW?

When Joshua Kimmich's transfer to Bayern Munich was being discussed in the summer of 2015, the Bavarian club dragged its feet. A higher up in the Munich establishment was unconvinced by the young Rottweiler. German football legend Karl-Heinz Rummenigge was sceptical about the young German yet Kimmich turned out to be a bargain, costing Bayern less than €10 million.

Presnel

KIMPEMBE

BORN: 13 August 1995
Beaumont-sur-Oise,
France

HEIGHT: 1.89 m

POSITION: Defender

PROFESSIONAL CAREER:
Paris Saint-Germain FC

Big meaty slaps on the thighs of Paul Pogba and Samuel Umtiti, the images seared into the minds of supporters. In the documentary *Les Bleus 2018, The Russian Epic* by Emmanuel Le Ber and Théo Schuster, the luxury joker Presnel Kimpembe teased two of the tricolour pillars of that success who sit and suffer in silence. Just like Benjamin Mendy's dancing, the reputation of the young Parisian defender was made, that of a playful boy loving life, certainly a joker but with an extraordinary mind.

His first trainers at PSG struggled to recognise the ability of the clumsy teenager who didn't really know what to do with his feet. Today, the player his partners call 'Presko'

exudes a rare serenity for a defender of his age. Nothing frightens him: he remedies any situation with a relaxed and calm air. In the absences of stars such as Thiago Silva or Marquinhos or in the event of the transfer of one of the two Brazilians, Presnel stood strong.

At the age of 24 the left-sided central defender was already a multi-champion of France with PSG, and despite a poor post–World Cup in 2018 he remained a safe bet in Ligue 1. With a constant desire to defend while remaining on his feet, the native of Beaumont-sur-Oise has valuable technical quality on each side. The kid from Éragny, a town in Val-d'Oise where he grew up, had come a long way.

Despite some setbacks Presnel Kimpembe gritted his teeth. 'I have always believed in myself. With the club, it was complicated but I hung on,' the Ile-de-France resident recalled. An adept at pressing, he convinced Laurent Blanc to launch him into the fray, the boss giving a vote of confidence to the elegant defender. Unai Emery also reinforced Presnel's conviction to go into battle relentlessly.

If all was well at the start with Thomas Tuchel, the German coach did not appreciate the opinion of Presnel Kimpembe. Following the Champions League elimination at the hands of Manchester United on away goals, Tuchel questioned the quality of the Parisian group. Kimpembe had actually scored his first professional goal at Old Trafford in the first leg. It may have brought controversy, but the speech nevertheless corresponded to the character of an endearing boy.

KIMPEMBE

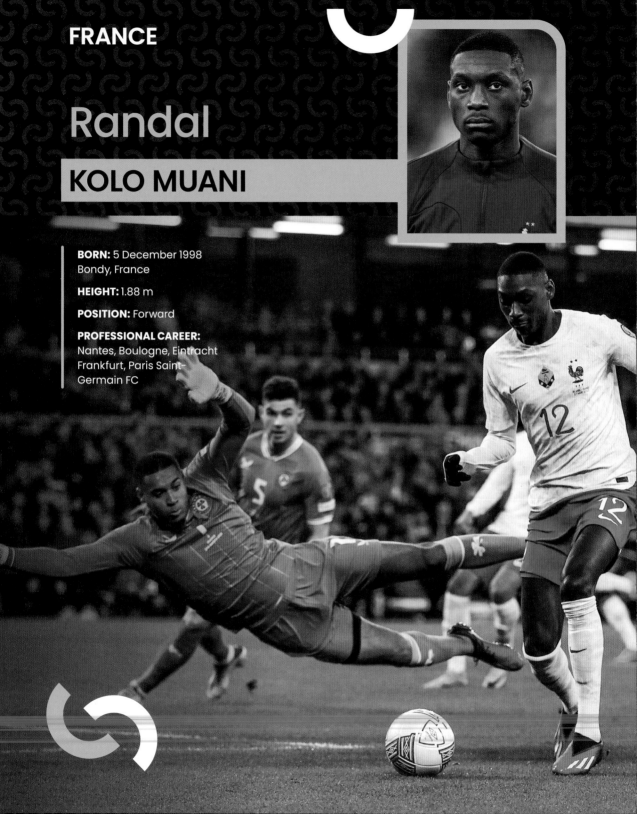

FRANCE

Randal
KOLO MUANI

BORN: 5 December 1998
Bondy, France

HEIGHT: 1.88 m

POSITION: Forward

PROFESSIONAL CAREER:
Nantes, Boulogne, Eintracht
Frankfurt, Paris Saint-
Germain FC

O n 18 December 2022 in Qatar in Lusail Stadium, which had already borne witness to one of the most epic football contests in history and had the watching crowd breathless, Argentina and France were deadlocked at 3–3 after 120 minutes of end-to-end exhilarating action in the FIFA World Cup final. As the seconds ticked away to the inevitable penalty shoot-out, a long ball from Ibrahima Konaté split the Argentine defence. Suddenly, Randal Kolo Muani found himself free, bearing down one on one with Argentina goalkeeper Emiliano Martínez. The forward had a fraction of a second to decide what to do as the custodian advanced, and his effort from the right of the area was superbly blocked by a player who would be named as the Golden Glove of the tournament.

It was harsh on a player who had made the difference for his team. Introduced in the 41st minute for Ousmane Dembélé, the French were adrift of their opponents, trailing 0–2 to a Leo Messi–inspired display and seemingly down and out, but Kolo Muani became the detonator of the unlikely comeback. It was he who won the penalty after being caught by Nicolás Otamendi, Kylian Mbappé doing the honours from the spot and reigniting hope in Les Bleus camp. However, it was not to be, and after the denouement of his saved chance Argentina won on penalties.

Far from destroying him psychologically, the former Nantes resident decided to use this mishap to bounce back. When he scored the opening goal against Morocco in the semi-finals, a 2–0 success, 'Kolo' found it hard to believe. It had taken an incredible combination of circumstances for him to even participate in the global fest. The career of the striker originally of Congolese culture has always had this taste for permanent miracles.

After developing at different clubs in the Parisian suburbs Randal got his foot in the door of training centres from Stéphanois and Rennes, but in vain. Nantes was the dream outcome but, here again, the future was darkening. Immature, Kolo was late for training most of the time so the Canaries staff sent him to toughen up at US Boulogne in the rough national championship. His return to Nantes was a success, punctuated by the Coupe de France win in 2022. The striker set sail to the Bundesliga the following summer, joining Eintracht Frankfurt. In a sensational debut year he played 53 matches, scoring 24 goals and creating 15 others. This led to a move back to France and the bright lights of the capital, joining PSG, where the next chapter of his career awaits.

DID YOU KNOW?

For his first match in the Bundesliga on 5 August 2022, Randal Kolo Muani experienced a disastrous baptism of fire. At Deutsche Bank Park in Frankfurt, the stronghold of European banks, Bayern Munich went to the cash register. Benjamin Pavard was among the goal scorers as Munich triumphed 6–1, Frankfurt's new number 9 finding the net in response on debut. It was of scant consolation, but it was a sign of things to come for the French striker.

KOLO MUANI

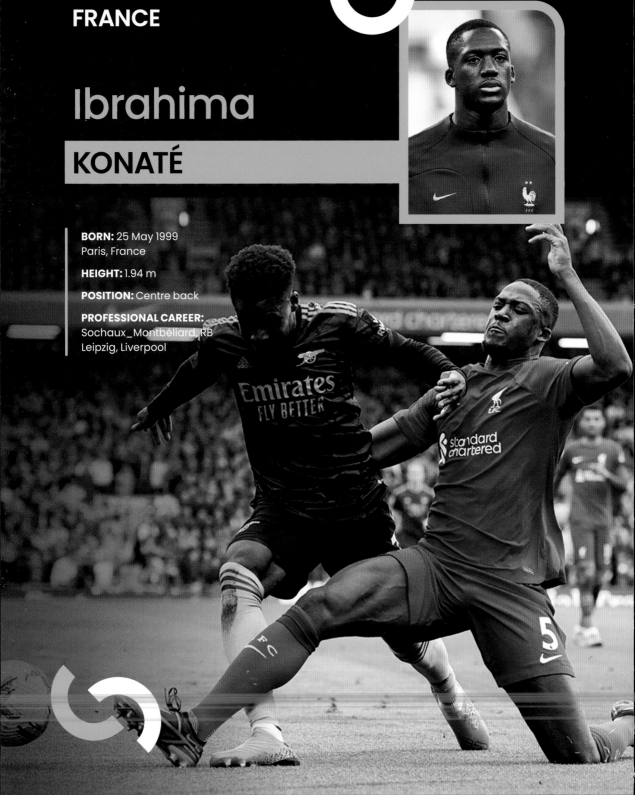

FRANCE

Ibrahima
KONATÉ

BORN: 25 May 1999
Paris, France

HEIGHT: 1.94 m

POSITION: Centre back

PROFESSIONAL CAREER:
Sochaux_Montbéliard, RB
Leipzig, Liverpool

On the grounds of Melwood in the suburbs of Liverpool, 'Ibou' rolled his eyes. 'In the early days I looked around me: it was incredible. In the locker room to my right was Virgil van Dijk [and] to my left Thiago Alcântara. They are guys I play with on FIFA!' When he arrived with the Reds in the summer of 2021 Ibrahima Konaté, on top of his game at just 22 years of age, had every reason to be impressed. However, the young Parisian of Malian origin is rarely flustered by his surroundings. It helped that his new coach, German Jürgen Klopp, was already a huge fan. 'I'm really happy that we were able to add Ibrahima to our team,' Klopp said. 'His physical qualities are very impressive: he is fast, very strong and dominant in the air.'

Having begun his career training and playing with Sochaux, starting with the team's reserves the Lion Cubs, Ibou did not arrive at Liverpool in unfamiliar territory: the previous four seasons had been spent in the demanding level of the Bundesliga alongside his compatriot Dayot Upamecano at RB Leipzig. Despite the impressive surroundings of Anfield, Konaté blended into the tradition of the club seamlessly and put himself in the pocket of the public who worship at the cathedral on the banks of the Mersey. When his family joined him, everyone was amazed by the ease of his adaptation. He quickly became a benchmark defender: a function that the Franco-Malian has not always held since, because as a teenager he played attack.

It was Reda Bekhti at Paris FC who took him back a notch, setting him up as a sentinel of the back. Then, looping in with his training in Franche-Comté near the Bonal Stadium, Konaté developed into a centre back of incredible power. With such a background and seeing a player who was certainly still juvenile but already endowed with vast experience, Didier Deschamps could not remain indifferent at national level.

To compensate for the absence of Raphaël Varane, in June 2022 Deschamps called Konaté up for the Nations League and Ibou debuted in Vienna, alongside William Saliba in the middle of the defence, in a 1–1 draw against Austria. Less than six months later came the adventure in Qatar during the FIFA World Cup, in which the Parisian defender appeared five times in seven matches. The kid from La Roquette, in the 11th district of the capital, came close to the Holy Grail against Argentina. He felt that the defeat was just a postponement: the future belongs to him.

KONATÉ

DID YOU KNOW?

Son Goku wants to save the world, and the hero of Dragon Ball inspires Ibrahima Konaté. A Manga fan, the French defender does not hide the fact that he sometimes projects himself in the manner of this Japanese comic book hero. 'His mentality inspires me enormously,' Konaté said. 'I don't look at my competitors; I focus on my own person and seek to reach the best possible level.' That's no problem as long as he doesn't fly to Vegeta, the planet where his favourite characters live . . .

SENEGAL

Kalidou

KOULIBALY

BORN: 20 June 1991
Saint-Dié-des-Vosges,
Senegal

HEIGHT: 1.87 m

POSITION: Defender

PROFESSIONAL CAREER:
FC Metz, KRC Genk,
SSC Naples, Chelsea FC,
Al Hilal SFC

Originally from Matam in Senegal, Kalidou Koulibaly's parents moved to Lorraine in France after the future superstar's father worked stoically for five years to save enough money for the move. Little Kalidou was born there in 1991. 'When you grow up in this environment, you see everyone as your brother,' he said. 'We are black, white, Arab, African, Muslim, Christian, yes – but we are all French.' Saint-Dié-des-Vosges remains in his heart: the community of this African ethnic group is important in the quiet city of the Vosges, but Koulibaly has a wider-reaching view of his place in the world.

Proud of his Senegalese origins, the future Lion of Teranga maintained a sincere attachment to the land of his origin, and his association with his international team shows that. 'When I find myself with my parents in the region of Fouta I am seen as a Frenchman. In France I am seen as a Senegalese. Everyone reminds you of where you come from,' Koulibaly said, ensuring that he places himself in this double culture that he is naturally proud of.

The footballer leaves the psychological, political and moral barriers to others unless it's a cause close to his heart. During a match played in Milan in December 2018 against Inter he was the victim of racist taunts from the stands of the Giuseppe Meazza stadium. The Senegalese man mountain ironically applauded the referee for his inaction. Warned for this gesture, before being sent off Koulibaly said he was 'proud of the colour of his skin' while refusing to argue. That's not his style. The wound, though, runs deep for the former adopted Neapolitan, who was immersed in an Italy that is too often behind the times in this area.

However, despite this he became an essential pawn among the Napoli defensive set-up. He is a giant with legs of velvet who is able to play in a relaxed and composed style and with a prodigious leap, regularly hoisting his 1.86 m frame nearly 2.5 m from the ground – like the spring day in 2018 in Turin when he scored a memorable and decisive goal with his head against a Juventus team who, up until that point, had been untouchable at home.

A high-flying champion, Kalidou nevertheless remains humble in any circumstance. His Chelsea tenure was often a struggle, and the big defender will be seeking to rediscover his form at Al Hilal in Saudi Arabia.

OU
N?

baly has
egalese
al since
er 2015.
st player
ed in the
0 team,
er finally
e Lions of
was my
ade me
ing me
d make
s proud
enough
tars in
es.'

Jules

KOUNDÉ

BORN: 12 November 1998
Paris, France

HEIGHT: 1.84 m

POSITION: Defender

PROFESSIONAL CAREER:
Bordeaux, Séville FC,
FC Barcelona

Everywhere and nowhere at the same time. Versatility is sometimes a naughty word, but you won't hear any complaints from Jules Koundé. If he plays centrally in his club team or he's deployed wider out in the colours of his national squad it matters little to this composed defender, who imposes himself on the action wherever he is selected.

Nicknamed the 'quiet strength' by those around him, Koundé was thrown into the deep end of the professional game by Jocelyn Gourvennec one evening in January 2018 in Granville, during a Coupe de France match that was played in nightmare conditions. In the wind and rain, and seeing his team reduced to nine men after two players were sent off, he was one of the few to emerge with any credit. The experience was tough but he validated his place in the team, a single appearance enough to establish his presence as an essential element of the Girondins Bordeaux defence in Ligue 1.

Born in Paris, little Koundé grew up in Gironde in Landiras in the middle of the Graves vineyards. Let go by Sochaux-Montbéliard but spotted via Bordeaux, he went through the stages of progression at his own pace. He was captain of the Bordeaux U-19 team, champions of France in 2017, but was snubbed by French youth teams up to the U-20s. It's a path that is a mirror of the image he portrays: that of a peaceful, discreet but assertive character.

Bordeaux managed to keep him for another season (70 matches, 4 goals in total) but finally let him go to Sevilla FC in the summer of 2019 for a substantial sum for a player of this age: €25 million.

With the French U-21 team Koundé was captain of the team in all eight of the matches he played in before he came knocking on the door of the first team, in contention for the Euro 2020 squad. His assurance and application in training were enough to convince Didier Deschamps that he could play a role in the European championship beyond being simply a top-class addition to a stacked bench.

He made his debut on 2 June 2021 in a friendly against Wales, coming on for left back Benjamin Pavard at half-time, and started the Nations League final win over Spain that same year. It was a meteoric rise, and things accelerated even more following this success as the world's biggest clubs came sniffing around. Eventually, he took the plunge and elected for a shift to Xavi's Barça in 2022. A new era awaits.

DID YOU KNOW?

In every locker room each player has their own nickname, and Jules Koundé is no exception to the rule. In his club in Seville he earned the nickname 'Cafu'! The Frenchman doesn't really know why but it doesn't matter, as he says the old captain of the Seleção was a legend. Koundé adapted perfectly to being nicknamed by the name of the Brazilian great by putting in a string of sensational performances.

Toni

KROOS

BORN: 4 January 1990
Greifswald, Germany

HEIGHT: 1.83 m

POSITION: Midfielder

PROFESSIONAL CAREER:
Bayern Munich,
Bayer 04 Leverkusen,
Bayern Munich,
Real Madrid

Toni Kroos is the archetypal essential player you only see the importance of, and the balance they bring to the team, when they are absent. Without him the German national team, like his club Real Madrid, loses discipline, physical resistance and impact.

More than just playing a sentinel role, the Pomeranian genius, born in the former German Democratic Republic two months after the fall of the Berlin Wall, shines in his role as a key cog in midfield. With his rigorous approach and analytical view of the game Toni has all the skills to be a vital part in any variable tactical formation, according to what is selected by his coaches.

At Real he is even able to cover the two wingers, who tend to be quick to project themselves forward and to sometimes forget the defensive tasks. A real engine in the heart of the game, the German also has another secret weapon: the millimetric precision of his right foot on passes or set pieces.

Despite the failure of the Nationalmannschaft at the 2018 World Cup, no one could forget Toni's goal from an amazing free kick against Sweden that gave Germany a win in added time. Unfortunately, they crashed out at the group stage. A jewel in the middle of a Scandinavian performance of some quality, with Sweden dominating, here was proof of his incredible determination.

In the first period a misplaced pass from Kroos meant Sweden was able to open the scoring through Ola Toivonen. With experience and pride, the 'Server' – Toni's nickname among German supporters – was able to recover. He continued to regulate the play, dictate the rhythm to his pace and set the right tempo, managing the best time to attempt a breach of a stern Swedish defence. During this match statistics showed that Kroos became the German player to have touched the ball most in a World Cup match since records began: he had more than 140 possessions of the ball.

At the Merengues he is the ideal complement to Luka Modrić for his construction of attacks. Besides, his precious curling crosses have long benefited Cristiano Ronaldo, and even today French striker Karim Benzema. In short, in the art of orientation and possession of the ball Toni Kroos has few peers.

KROOS

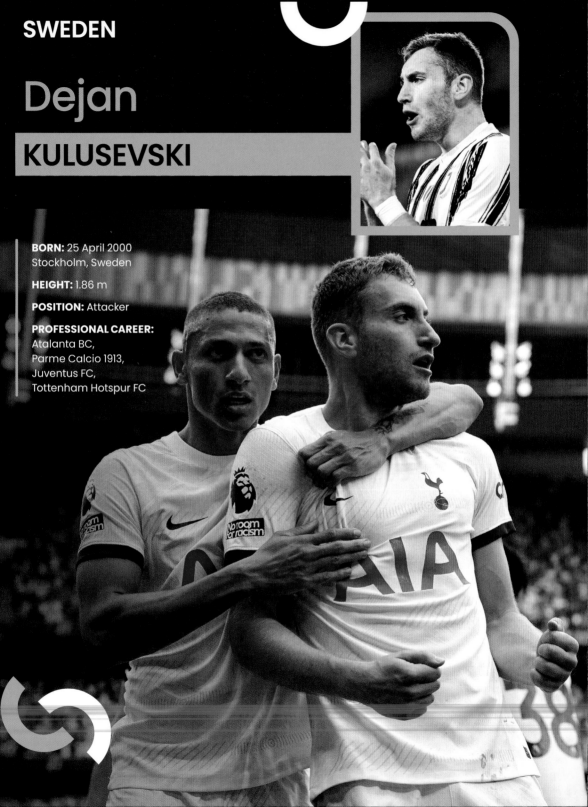

SWEDEN

Dejan

KULUSEVSKI

BORN: 25 April 2000
Stockholm, Sweden

HEIGHT: 1.86 m

POSITION: Attacker

PROFESSIONAL CAREER:
Atalanta BC,
Parme Calcio 1913,
Juventus FC,
Tottenham Hotspur FC

nevitably, the comparison is made on a systematic and regular basis: originally from the Balkans and Viking by adoption, could Dejan Kulusevski be the new Zlatan? Although Ibrahimović was one of his idols when he grew up in the Vällingby district, on the walls of his bedroom the wallpaper was covered instead by Ronaldinho posters. If there is a sporting comparison to be made on the field, it is obvious that Kulusevski has more of the genius of the Brazilian than of the giant of Malmö. And if 'Ibra' has never tried the international adventure in the Bosnian jersey, Kulusevski got closer to the federation of his origin – Macedonia – at a younger age by agreeing to play five matches in the red jersey of the national U-16 team.

His early years at IF Brommapojkarna confirmed his hopes. He perfected his technique in futsal during the endless Scandinavian winter months. He is a pure box-to-box player with an ability to move from goal to goal. Arsenal came looking, but the director of the academy of Bergamo, Maurizio Costanzi, was the more prompt in allowing Atalanta to steal the prodigy. It took just three years for Dejan Kulusevski to start with the primavera team, being called up in January 2019 under the orders of Gian Piero Gasperini.

The boy brought comparisons to Mo Salah. Like the Egyptian, the promising Swede has the power at any time to make the difference and is lightning over 10 m. 'Shady' loves to play on the right side, before cutting infield to better allow his devastating left foot to do its work. He was loaned to Parma to gain playing time and there his reputation in Italy swelled, in particular thanks to his capacity to create opportunities for others, racking up a number of assists with his decisive passes. Suddenly, Kulusevski was attracting the big names of Serie A, especially after he was awarded a maiden Swedish international cap in November 2019.

It was ultimately Juventus who lured him to their ranks, a further comparison coming when his scurrying style and slender frame recalled that of Eden Hazard. This was not surprising: in his first match he opened the scoring against Sampdoria with a beautifully controlled free kick. At the end of his first year in Turin he was named Best Young Player in Serie A. A harder time followed, and Kulusevski is looking to rebuild his career at Tottenham Hotspur.

KULUSEVSKI

DID YOU KNOW?

Having barely landed at Juventus, Dejan Kulusevski showed a lot of nerve. During an interview granted to a Swedish television station the young winger lent himself to a game of express questions, and when the journalist asked him 'Messi or Cristiano Ronaldo?' the ambitious hopeful made a response citing the name of the Argentinian. On the Turin side the fans were the most saddened, and if the Italian press were sensing a scandal they were quickly disappointed. CR7 did not take offence.

GEORGIA

Khvicha

KVARATSKHELIA

BORN: 12 February 2001
Tbilisi, Georgia

HEIGHT: 1.83 m

POSITION: Winger

PROFESSIONAL CAREER:
FC Dinamo Tbilisi,
FC Rustavi, FC Lokomotiv
Moscow, FC Rubin Kazan,
FC Dinamo Batumi,
SSC Napoli

Nicknamed 'Kvaradona' by Neapolitan supporters, the Georgian left winger could have suffered when he arrived at the foot of Vesuvius in July 2022. Imagine the dilemma for the child of Nakifu, just 22 years old and already being compared with the absolute icon Diego Armando Maradona. Khvicha melted into the Gli Azzurri collective with foolproof insurance. The challenge was even more difficult to take on because on this left flank he had to succeed Lorenzo Insigne, who had gone into exile at Toronto FC. The result just 10 months later was that he was one of the main players in the conquest of a third Scudetto for Napoli, which had not had its paws on the Italian Serie A title for 33 years!

What an incredible journey for this slender boy, whose main strength is his quality of striking with both feet and his technical ease, confusing defenders with his wily dribbles and rapid changes of direction. The least we can say is that the path taken by this little genius of the round ball was not linear. After having done his classes in the local championship and with a 2018–19 season at FC Roustavi, Khvicha seemed well on his way to a career in Russia. First loaned to Lokomotiv Moscow, the Georgian winger was then transferred to Rubin Kazan. However, in March 2022, after the invasion of Ukraine, he was forced to quickly flee.

Becoming an international and with his reputation reinforced in status by the Frenchman Willy Sagnol, the tightrope walker from Tbilisi refound his feet with a short stint back in his homeland at Dinamo Batumi. To everyone's surprise the Neapolitan leaders put their hands on this nugget, who became the first Georgian to put on the sky-blue jersey. The Neapolitan coach Luciano Spalletti was amazed by his ability to counterattack and constantly vary his offensive options.

His understanding with striker Victor Osimhen was one of the secrets of the success of this Napoli side that revelled in perpetual movement. 'He has one technique worthy of the strongest in the world and this quality of feeling where the goal is to always create the best chances,' insisted Spalletti, talking about a player who always puts him in the best mood. After the surprise effect of his first months, Khvicha continues to confirm his enormous potential and continues to delight his fans.

DID YOU KNOW?

The Georgian left winger could have played in Ligue 1, but the many French club directors were panicked by his surname! If Willy Sagnol whispered his name to a few presidents of clubs, no one took the risk of betting on this reinforcement. 'I was even asked to find a Latin nickname for Kvaratskhelia,' revealed the outraged ex–Bayern Munich and French national team defender.

KVARATSKHELIA

Aymeric

LAPORTE

BORN: 27 May 1994
Agen, France

HEIGHT: 1.91 m

POSITION: Defender

PROFESSIONAL CAREER:
Athletic Bilbao,
Manchester City FC,
Al-Nassr FC

He is French, but there is not much in the world of football that ties Aymeric Laporte to the country of his birth. If you look carefully, maybe his first steps in the youth set-up of Agen or in Bayonne at the regional level among other young hopefuls. The rest is an accumulation of experiences, of missed appointments with French clubs. Whose fault is that? Even Aymeric would struggle to answer that question himself.

At the age of 12 he packed his backpack for Spain, having been spotted by Athletic Bilbao during a match with the regional team of Aquitaine. His move prompted much debate among locals due to their strict Basque-only policy at the time. In Bilbao he entered another world, but the young Frenchman learned quickly and settled well. He made steady progress in the region, eventually becoming an indispensable member of the team.

It was evident that Bilbao was becoming too small for him, and even though Barcelona were casting covetous eyes his way it was 'Goodbye, Spain' as big-spending Manchester City came calling and won the race for his signature. The adopted Spaniard left the country that saw him grow up as a footballer and that vigorously flirted with him for national team selection.

Laporte had always remained faithful to the Blues of France in the youth categories and was looked at by Didier Deschamps, but after several misunderstandings and injuries that curtailed his involvement he was still uncapped at senior level by the team with the rooster on their chest. Indeed, his relationship with Coach Deschamps grew complicated. Left out of the squad for Euro 2016 in France and the victorious World Cup campaign in Russia two years later, he was called up again but an untimely injury prevented him from joining the team at Clairefontaine.

Laporte appeared destined never to play for France so it was perhaps a little surprising when he finally chose Spain, for whom he made a convincing debut just before Euro 2020 in a friendly with Iberian neighbours Portugal. Never a first choice for France, it was quite the opposite with Pep Guardiola at the Citizens. The Catalan boss had long been an admirer of Laporte and for €65 million the English club snapped up their man, making him the second-most expensive defender in history in 2018.

At that price Laporte proved worth it and more, winning everything there was to win in City Blue and culminating in the treble, before deciding to join the exodus to Saudi Arabia, signing for Al-Nassr alongside Cristiano Ronaldo.

LAPORTE

DID YOU KNOW?

Everything led all to believe that Aymeric Laporte would score tries rather than goals. Originally from Agen, a city in the south-west of France where rugby is king, he has never been attracted by the oval ball despite his father having been a rugby player in the second division. 'My father didn't want me to play rugby because he thought it was very hard on the body, so at school I was more into football and that's where it all started.'

POLAND

Robert

LEWANDOWSKI

BORN: 21 August 1988
Varsovie, Poland

HEIGHT: 1.85 m

POSITION: Striker

PROFESSIONAL CAREER:
Znicz Pruszków,
Lech Poznań,
Borussia Dortmund,
Bayern Munich,
FC Barcelona

DID YOU KNOW?

On 9 March 2019 Bayern Munich pulverised VfL Wolfsburg 6–0. During the game Robert Lewandowski scored twice, and with 197 goals since his Bundesliga debut in 2010 became the all-time top foreign goal scorer, beating the target set by the Peruvian Claudio Pizarro 0f 195 goals. He netted his 200th league goal in a 5–0 win over Dortmund a month later.

H e could have been seen him in the Tour de France: a big bike lover since he was a kid, Robert Lewandowski put on cycling gear as soon as he had the opportunity to do so in the Bavarian countryside. A sports enthusiast, the Polish striker also indulged in bodybuilding sessions in a furnished room of his villa. Well, as you might understand, Oktoberfest in Germany is not really his thing! A healthy body and a healthy mind: in October 2017 'Lewy' earned a sports management degree. His thesis, 'RL9, path to glory', pleased his fans, who on this occasion were dressed in red and white and had a history of paying homage to their prestigious student.

Lewandowski had an incredible journey to the top flight and its riches, a story that began 10 years earlier as a professional at Znicz Pruszków, in the midst of Mazovia, earning just €500 per month. Some months previously his football career had been almost nipped in the bud when, as a young hopeful at Legia Warszawa, he was unceremoniously fired from the great club of the Polish capital. 'Not tough enough,' they said. Moreover, the teenager had a rather suspect knee, which led the Legia doctors to finding him fragile.

With a mother who was a volleyball player and a dad who practised judo, Lewandowski was blessed with the DNA of a future champion. His career exploded into life at Lech Poznań and then in Germany, where the world began to sit up and take notice of Lewy's prodigious scoring feats.

In the 2010 off-season Borussia Dortmund won the race to snag his signature and so began a decade rich in exploits in the Bundesliga. The Pole is the archetypal centre forward of modern times: strong on both feet, dexterous in the air and with an unexpected versatility.

During his time on the bench of Bayern Munch, the club that took Lewandowski from Dortmund, Pep Guardiola even developed him into an unexpected left winger!

Lewandowski doesn't shirk his defensive responsibilities either, but it's in front of goal that he set record after record with his incredible run of goals at the Bavarian giants. If there is one blight on his career it was arguably his limited impact at major tournaments with Poland. However, he did break his World Cup scoring duck at the 2022 edition in Qatar and hit the ground running amid a blaze of goals at Barcelona, a new chapter in his goal-laden career.

LEWANDOWSKI

FRANCE

Hugo

LLORIS

BORN: 26 December 1986
Nice, France

HEIGHT: 1.88 m

POSITION: Goalkeeper

PROFESSIONAL CAREER:
OGC Nice,
Olympique Lyonnaise,
Tottenham Hotspur FC, Los
Angeles FC

DID YOU KNOW?

Hugo Lloris did not always want to be a footballer. Before stopping the balls on the pitch he was passionate about tennis. He was even ranked among the best nationals during his childhood, and it's a tiny bit thanks to tennis that he began playing football. 'I started in football thanks to my tennis club,' he said. 'I was spending most of my weekends there with my parents. I met up with my friends and we alternated [between] football and tennis.'

lowly, surely and quietly, the captain of Les Bleus built his legend in the French team. Setting the record for matches played by a goalkeeper for France and as captain for the national team, with each passing match Hugo Lloris consolidated a little more his place in the history books. After the statistics, two images stick long in the memory preserved for posterity: that amazing reflex save on his line against Cáceres of Uruguay in the quarter final of the 2018 World Cup, and a day of glory against Croatia. It was Lloris who, on 15 July 2018, lifted the World Cup to the heavens as captain of the side that achieved global dominance. It was a second world title for France, 20 years after that of coach Didier Deschamps.

Lloris had come a long way since Knysna! In South Africa, in a shameful display by France, his dreams of glory went up in smoke. He was marked by this episode and worked for a new state of mind without ever giving up. It's a strength of Lloris, who is globally and undisputedly respected for his performances by those sitting alongside him in the national team changing rooms.

In the intimate surrounds of this group Lloris, the quiet person, can turn into a vocal and committed leader ready to express the truth of his performances. An exemplary leader of the world champions for four years, it was a relief for Lloris to add a more substantial trophy to the one he snatched from third division US Quevilly in the Coupe de France final in 2012 while playing for Lyon.

A move to Tottenham Hotspur in the English Premier League followed in 2012, but it was far from an unblemished transition. Lloris endured six complicated months upon his arrival at White Hart Lane, a period when Brad Friedel relegated him to a watching brief. In trouble in England, he didn't lose his status in the France team and the difficult start was quickly forgotten. His improved performances and leadership qualities saw him take over the skipper's armband at Spurs.

Captain of his country and now his club: it was anything but a coincidence: the Frenchman is a born leader of men. 'He's the best goalkeeper in the world,' his coach Mauricio Pochettino, after a sensational display against Ajax Amsterdam in the Champions League semi-finals, exclaimed. Playing in the Champions League final against Liverpool, there was nothing the Tottenham keeper could do about either of the Reds goals. Lloris's shot at glory for the cup with the big ears will have to wait.

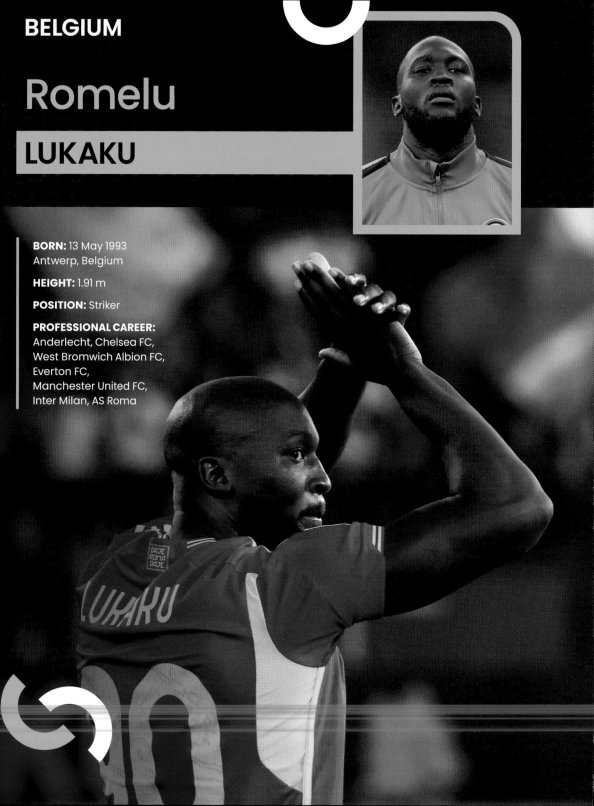

BELGIUM

Romelu

LUKAKU

BORN: 13 May 1993
Antwerp, Belgium

HEIGHT: 1.91 m

POSITION: Striker

PROFESSIONAL CAREER:
Anderlecht, Chelsea FC,
West Bromwich Albion FC,
Everton FC,
Manchester United FC,
Inter Milan, AS Roma

When young, Romelu Lukaku never thought of being a football star. The kid from Antwerp had an old head on young shoulders, and despite being ahead of his peers on the pitch he just wanted to play football and enjoy himself on the field. False modesty, or a lack of ambition? Probably the former, as Lukaku is the top scorer in the history of the Belgian national team, having netted 68 goals in 104 internationals at the culmination of the 2022 FIFA World Cup in Qatar.

As a child he already dreamed of annihilating his opponents. 'I was trying to rip the leather off the ball every time I kicked it. No finesse shooting. I wasn't kidding. I was trying to kill you.'

While not always orthodox in this technique, Lukaku is not just a man mountain and a huge physical specimen ready to bulldoze his way to individual glory. Indeed, he is more of an altruistic centre forward, wedded to the good of the team. It's in his nature.

A difficult childhood in the middle of a penniless family for whom the electricity bills each month proved to be a headache inspired a driving force to achieve. In a confession published on The Players' Tribune website, the ex–Manchester United player described a daily life of poverty. One anecdote from when he was aged six left a telling mark: 'I caught my mother adding water to my bowl of milk,' Lukaku remembered. 'The same as the day before. I realised then that we were broke. Not just poor: broke. That day I knew exactly what I had to do and what I was going to do.'

From there it was a goal-laden story, with bags of goals wherever the left footer took his 1.91 m and 94 kg frame. His first professional contract was with Belgian side Anderlecht, signing for the perennial Belgian champions when he had just turned 16. After winning the Belgian title and scooping the top scorer gong, the striker was on the move to England.

Not really given much of a chance at Chelsea, he exploded at Everton with 87 goals in four seasons, awakening the interest of the big Premier League clubs. A switch to Manchester United yielded 42 goals in 96 appearances before Lukaku headed to Italy and a prolific spell with Internazionale. Latterly, he made a brief return to Chelsea before re-signing on loan with Inter. A tumultuous summer followed for the big striker in 2023 before he ended up in Rome as part of José Mourinho's rebuild at AS Roma.

DID YOU KNOW?

A true force of nature, Romelu Lukaku experienced very rapid growth. He was already so big and massive as a child that he had to constantly justify his age in the youth categories. His first trainer, Erwin Wosky, recalled it well: 'At nine years old he already had adult shoes. The coaches did not believe that he was that young; he had to carry his passport everywhere with him to prove it. The other children literally started crying when they saw him coming. He was a monster.'

ALGERIA

Riyad

MAHREZ

BORN: 21 February 1991
Sarcelles, France

HEIGHT: 1.79 m

POSITION: Winger

PROFESSIONAL CAREER:
Quimper Kerfeunteun FC,
Le Havre AC, Leicester City FC,
Manchester City FC,
Al-Ahli Saudi FC

At first glance, the story of Riyad Mahrez looks like so many others: that of a kid from a working-class neighborhood where talents compete with each other – except that for the Algerian international his talent was not obvious. He was just an ordinary young man, a technical player like the Parisian suburbs offer in abundance. Born in Sarcelles and trained in Quimper, Mahrez needed to move to be given the opportunity to shine.

'When Quimper offered me a trial [in 2009] I was 18 years old,' Mahrez recalled. 'The train ticket cost €160. I said to my mother: "Don't worry, I'll give it back to you, I'll make it".' Nine years later Manchester City signed a cheque for €68 million to recruit the kid from Val-d'Oise.

From his professional beginnings in Le Havre to becoming a superstar in England, the course that Mahrez took was far from straightforward. While he dreamed of joining Olympique Marseille, the team he supported as a youth, there were more than a few doubts about making the switch from Le Harve to Leicester City in 2014. For him, Leicester was synonymous with rugby union! It's fair to say then that it wasn't for the love of the jersey that Mahrez joined the Foxes, yet at the club in the middle of England he won the Premier League title and was voted best player in the competition in 2016. The surprise of the century was signed and sealed with a combination of Jamie Vardy and the enigmatic Mahrez.

Everyone now knows that there is more to Leicester than the oval ball game. The individual awards began to stack up, and Mahrez was announced as the Confederation of African Football's Footballer of the Year. A big move to Manchester City followed and he began to add more medals to an impressive collection. In 2019, in an exceptional season, he also became an African Cup of Nations winner with Algeria. The Fennecs made the final on the back of an injury-time winner in the semi-final from Mahrez – a brilliant free kick – before being crowned continental champions with a 1–0 win over Senegal. Twenty-nine years after Rabah Madjer, Algerian football had found a new icon.

Riyad Mahrez could have played for France, but the Algerian Football Federation had already eyed him off and tied him to them before the 2014 FIFA World Cup. Mahrez's career took a new direction in 2023–24 when he left Manchester City to pursue a fresh adventure with crack Saudi Arabian outfit Al-Ahli.

DID YOU KNOW?

Before blazing a trail in England Riyad Mahrez was offered to Marseille in the winter of 2014, but the president of the Marseille club, Vincent Labrune, rejected the opportunity to sign the Algerian striker. When Mahrez's agent emailed him to offer him Riyad and Zinedine Ferhat, a raw talent from the Algerian championship, Labrune's response a few hours later was scathing. 'Do you really think players from Leicester and USM Algiers can have their place at OM in our project?' he wrote. That looks a bit silly now.

Sadio

MANÉ

BORN: 10 April 1992
Sedhiou, Senegal

HEIGHT: 1.75 m

POSITION: Forward

PROFESSIONAL CAREER:
FC Metz, RB Salzbourg,
Southampton FC,
Liverpool FC,
Bayern Munich,
Al-Nassr FC

The party could not take place because the coronavirus had made its appearance, but the 19th League title won by Liverpool in 2019–20 was nonetheless marked by celebrations. This was a release for the Reds, their first top-flight crown in the Premier League era since the redesign in 1992 and the first title since 1990.

Sadio Mané entered into the history of the club with some stunning achievements on the field and some eye-catching statistical records. In September 2019 in the 3–0 victory at Anfield against Newcastle United, not only did Mané net a double but he also became the first Premier League player to play 50 games at home without losing a single one! With 41 victories racked up and just nine draws, alongside 35 goals scored plus seven assists, his record was impressive.

Having arrived quietly at Anfield the African striker was suddenly essential, and especially since the combination of a front three with Mohamed Salah and Roberto Firmino constituted one of the most formidable offensive trios in England. An introverted person, Sadio Mané has forged a character that appears to be made of reinforced concrete. He wants to succeed – he must succeed – and the round-ball game has given him a chance to do just that.

Enlisted in 2005 at Académie Génération Foot, a training centre of FC Metz in Dakar, the future hero of Casamance flourished. On the ground opponents soon learned that it was better not to let him pick up speed, especially since it was impossible to read his intentions. The unpredictable Senegalese can both go on the outside before crossing or cut inside to strike. It's an eternal dilemma for defenders, since Sadio is as skilful with his left foot as he is with his right. To top it all off, he's not too bad in the air and his defensive application is not negligible either. He is an almost perfect player.

After showing his potential at FC Metz, two seasons later Mané was part of transfer to Red Bull Salzburg that precipitated an incredible transfer tale. In moving to Austria he subsequently became the most expensive African player in history, at €41 million when he moved in 2016 from Southampton to Liverpool. He left Merseyside to join Bayern Munich in 2022 before surprisingly joining Saudi Arabian Pro League side Al-Nassr after completing just one season in Bavaria.

MANÉ

DID YOU KNOW?

Sadio Mané could have become a Gunner. In 2012 and while FC Metz was ensconced in the National League, Mané seemed to be at an impasse. The president of Generation Foot, Mady Touré, remained close to the Senegalese striker and offered him to Gilles Grimandi, one of Arsenal's scouts at the time. The verdict was a bitter blow for the young forward from Sédhiou: his potential was considered to be 'too insufficient'. Without any hard feelings Sadio Mané later made that judgement appear ill-placed elsewhere in England.

BRAZIL

MARQUINHOS

BORN: 14 May 1994
São Paulo, Brazil

HEIGHT: 1.83 m

POSITION: Defender

PROFESSIONAL CAREER:
Corinthians SP, AS Roma,
Paris Saint-Germain FC

PSG sometimes looked like the Seleção: a colony of Brazilian internationals frequently seen dancing the samba in the French locker room. Neymar, Thiago Silva, Dani Alves ... but the best of them all was not necessarily the one grabbing the most headlines. However, this player was the most essential, most efficient one in the long term, rarely injured and always ready to play for the good of the team in a position that might not necessarily be his best. This is Marquinhos.

Marquinhos, whose real name is Marcos Aoás Corrêa, is a blessing for a coach: he is a discreet footballer with indisputable quality and incredible value. This is why every summer the biggest clubs – Juventus and FC Barcelona being just two to have shown interest – knock on the door of PSG to make an offer, which the Parisian club does not even consider. Marquinhos is not for sale at any price!

Equipped with an impressive maturity from an early age, Marquinhos is a complete central defender. Fast and efficient in his interceptions, the Brazilian has a rare sense of placement and an amazing vision of the game from his position as central defender. Looking back, in his life as a footballer everything happened very quickly. A professional at the age of 17 in the jersey of Corinthians of São Paulo, Marquinhos quickly went to Europe, to Roma, where he won the hearts of the supporters in double time. He even earned a first call-up for the Brazilian national team while he was still young enough to sport traces of acne on his face.

The big European clubs were courting him, and it was the Qatar-backed Paris Saint-Germain that raided the bank to secure his services for a cool €35 million. At that price some were saying only time would tell whether it was a good deal, and six years after his arrival in the French capital it can be ascertained that he was an absolute gift. Given the prices that defenders are beginning to attract, the fee is a steal.

Marquinhos soon became a regular member of the squad and an almost omnipresent figure in the national selection, from which he won the Olympic gold medal in Rio. He benefited from the presence of defensive colleague Miranda, who had been installed in the Seleção after the fiasco of the 2014 World Cup. With his impeccable French, Marquinhos is a potential captain near the Porte d'Auteuil, and while he may not be the flashiest Brazilian seen at the Parc des Princes he is a vital part of a star-studded line-up.

MARQUINHOS

DID YOU KNOW?

At the age of 25 Marquinhos was one of the best defenders in the world, but his fate could have been very different. The younger Marquinhos touched his first footballs as a goalkeeper playing in the small futsal club SACI, and according to his coaches at the time the lad was good in goal. However, one day he moved up the pitch to troubleshoot in defence, and the rest is known.

FRANCE

Anthony
MARTIAL

BORN: 5 December 1995
Massy, France

HEIGHT: 1.81 m

POSITION: Forward

PROFESSIONAL CAREER:
Olympique Lyonnais,
AS Monaco,
Manchester United FC

Eleven instead of 9: Anthony Martial bowed to the king's choice. When Zlatan Ibrahimović arrived at Manchester United in the summer of 2016 the Swedish giant railed against the fact that a young French international had stolen his favourite jersey number. So, without having been informed, the former Lyonnais attacker found himself decked out in number 11 for the Red Devils.

Some might have been stung by this and caused a scene, but that is not the style of the forward from Île-de-France. He believed he still had everything to prove in England and just got on with it. Since his first dribbles at Les Bergères, in the district of Les Ulis where he grew up, Anthony Martial made waves. Even then there was little chance of him being labelled a big head in spite of his stature. 'If I changed my big brothers [would] be the first to shoot me down,' Martial laughed.

From his early beginnings in the Lyon youth ranks, Martial's personality was difficult to fathom. His stare dark and deep, he rarely let any feelings show. Modest and discreet, the player that some observers dubbed the 'new Thierry Henry' kept his doubts and joys to himself. 'I am a calm, composed person who likes to laugh,' he admitted.

In England some find this lack of emotion hard to fathom: former Red Devils such as Paul Scholes are annoyed by his passivity. 'Martial, when he misses an opportunity, he is not angry at himself!' the United midfield legend lamented.

Transferred from AS Monaco to Manchester United in August 2015 for €80 million, the young man of Martinican origin did not back down from the magnitude of the task and lit up Old Trafford with a stunning solo goal on debut, as a substitute against United's traditional rivals Liverpool. Thanks to a few dazzling if irregular displays, the French star amazed the United faithful. 'Apart from the climate, I like everything about Manchester,' Martial said. 'People are respectful here.' The club was seduced by his audacity, and he frequently fractured opposing defences. Zlatan was able to enjoy his services first, then it was Romelu Lukaku's turn. 'On the left, I touch the ball a lot more. I can thus provoke and play on my qualities,' Martial explained.

Too quiet in his performances for the national team, he found his way barred by the Mbappé phenomenon ahead of the 2018 FIFA World Cup. As usual, without putting pressure on himself Anthony Martial merely shrugged and kept moving on.

DID YOU KNOW?

Anthony Martial's older brother Johan is also a professional player, as a central defender. After going through Bastia, Brest and Troyes, Johan decided to sign for an Israeli club in 2017 and joined the squad of Maccabi Petah Tikva. Selected for the French U-21 team, Johan finally strengthened the Martinican selection and even participated in the Gold Cup, the equivalent of the Euros in North America, Central America and the Caribbean.

Lautaro

MARTÍNEZ

BORN: 22 August 1997
Bahía Blanca, Argentina

HEIGHT: 1.74 m

POSITION: Striker

PROFESSIONAL CAREER:
Racing Club de Avellaneda,
FC Inter Milan

In the near future Lautaro Martínez could well be mentioned in the same breath as some of the greatest Argentinean goal scorers such as Mario Kempes and Carlos Tevez. Why? Because 'El Toro' is not only an incredible competitor who plays with physicality and aggressiveness but is also an amazing goal hunter. With these qualities he recalls a certain Gabriel Batistuta. Others find his a hybrid style between that of Gonzalo Higuaín and Sergio Agüero.

When during the Copa América 2019 no less than Lionel Messi dubbed this capable striker 'outstanding' thanks to his versatility to play in any system – as a pure centre forward, as part of a pair or even in support of the attacker – we are surely looking at a future superstar.

In December 2018 he entered the hearts of the tifosi of Internazionale in a clash against Napoli, scoring the only goal during additional time: an ideal scenario to ingratiate yourself with your supporters! Five months earlier for the sum of €23 million, Lautaro arrived in the capital of the Lombard region on the advice of Wanda Nara, wife of Mauro Icardi and incidentally a football agent. Lautaro arrived with a good reputation that had been fostered on the other side of the Atlantic.

At Racing Club, one of the many clubs in Buenos Aires, he shone like the light of a thousand fires in the jersey of the Academia. However, not everything was rosy in Argentina, because as a teenager Martínez had been released by Boca Juniors. The bitterness was huge, but he is stubborn. His father Mario, a former player himself, pushed young Lautaro on a daily basis. Mario had never been able to make the breakthrough but he believed in the destiny of his offspring.

Martínez was surprisingly good with his head for someone of modest size, and at Racing Club he even began as a defender. He soon moved further forward and, after 22 goals in 48 matches, alerted the presence of the European giants. Barça tried to recruit the little bull in 2018, but it was Inter who won the race for his signature.

Having made his Argentina debut in March 2018, Martínez netted the winning penalty in the 2022 FIFA World Cup quarter final shoot-out against the Netherlands, sending La Albiceleste into the semi-finals. From there, a World Cup winner with Argentina, he literally had the world at his feet.

DID YOU KNOW?

At the age of 18 Lautaro Martínez, with a tempered steel character, refused an offer from the prestigious Real Madrid club because he wanted to succeed first in the colours of Racing Club, notably in the Copa Libertadores, before leaving for Europe. This was an extremely rare fact that was revealed by the president of the Argentina team, Victor Blanco, in person, in the daily newspaper *Mundo Deportivo*.

FRANCE

Kylian

MBAPPÉ

BORN: 20 December 1998
Paris, France

HEIGHT: 1.78 m

POSITION: Forward

PROFESSIONAL CAREER:
AS Monaco,
Paris Saint-Germain FC

Born on 30 June 2018 even if, officially, Kylian Mbappé first saw the light of day on 20 December 1998. From a footballing point of view the planet discovered a little wonder on a warm Russian summer day in the Round of 16 at the World Cup. In Kazan Mbappé, a precocious attacker, disintegrated the Argentine defence with a dazzling display. In the 11th minute the boy from Bondy, the son of Fayza and Wilfrid, launched a dazzling counter.

Timed at 37 km/hour, 'Razmoket' ate up the ground before being illegally stopped by Marcos Rojo. The penalty was converted by Antoine Griezmann, which marked the beginning of a tricolour festival. The conclusion was a memorable success at 4–3 that was signed by a double from a kid just 19 years old.

Of course, Kylian Mbappé is no longer an unknown. From his debut with AS Monaco in the Champions League, the cream of European football – Manchester City, Borussia Dortmund, Juventus and the rest – found out about the audacity of the new pearl of French football. Besides his supersonic speed, Mbappé impressed with his maturity on the pitch. With an innate sense of realism and ice cold in front of goal, he tortured opposing goalkeepers.

It wasn't just on the pitch that he was impressive. The disconcerting young man showed remarkable calmness, his comments lucid and at ease in front of the microphone. He presented an intelligent persona, and Mbappé mania swept the globe. A world champion in 2018, scoring in the final win over Croatia and congratulated by King Pelé in person, Mbappé broke all youth records, and not just with his countless goals.

A record transfer to PSG in 2017 brought even more goals and accolades, but the pinnacle on a personal level was about to come. Qatar, 2022: a second FIFA World Cup final, and Mbappé became only the second man ever to net a hat-trick in a global showdown, following England's Geoff Hurst in 1966. His treble helped the game end 3–3, but it was to be Messi's coronation.

The heir apparent to the Argentine phenomenon, he already boasts 12 World Cup finals goals and four in the biggest game on the planet, the final itself. There's no telling where this journey may end.

DID YOU KNOW?

In the summer of 2011 Kylian Mbappé could have become Norman. On the wish list of Caen, the 13-year-old kid was already attracting covetous glances and the team from the Malherbe stadium was in the running. However, as they were in financial strife at the time the Calvados club tightened its belt and decided not to pay the €60,000 needed to recruit the AS Bondy prodigy; the president of Caen at the time, Jean-François Fortin, preferred to save jobs. Farewell, Kylian, and the young Parisian ended up at the Clairefontaine academy instead.

Édouard

MENDY

BORN: 1 March 1992
Montivilliers, France

HEIGHT: 1.94 m

POSITION: Goalkeeper

PROFESSIONAL CAREER:
AS Cherbourg,
Olympique de Marseille,
Stade de Reims,
Stade Rennais FC,
Chelsea FC,
Al-Ahli Saudi FC

Named best goalkeeper of the year in 2021 by UEFA, Édouard Mendy can be proud of his career – especially since beyond his exploits in goal at club level the Senegalese goalkeeper lifted the African Cup of Nations trophy in February 2022 when the Teranga Lions defeated Egypt in the final in Yaoundé, winning 4–2 on penalties after a 0–0 draw. In the aftermath of the match against the Pharaohs he was one of the main craftsmen behind the qualification of his team for the World Cup in Qatar.

This was a far cry from Le Havre where, two decades earlier, the kid from Montivilliers discovered the role of goalkeeper. The slender teenager had everything to break through but faced a circuitous route to do so. He first found himself at CS Municipal Services of Le Havre before joining Cherbourg, then in the national division. After the club was administratively downgraded to the Division d'Honneur Cherbourg found itself unable to pay its players, which meant that Édouard found himself unemployed.

For a short time he joined Olympique Marseille, playing in the B team and being an understudy to Franco–Senegalese goalkeepers Steve Mandanda and Yohann Pelé. It was Stade de Reims in 2016 that gave him his chance in Ligue 1. For three years Édouard reveled at Reims and became a well-respected custodian in France. He confirmed this impression when he transferred to Rennes for the 2019–20 season, when his presence between the posts and his reflex ability was reassuring to his defenders.

At Roazhon Park he also discovered the pleasure of battle in European games during evenings patrolling his area in the Europa League. In September 2020 the Normand crossed the channel and disembarked in London, where Chelsea offered him a five-year contract. Coach Frank Lampard gave him the number 1 spot at the expense of the Spaniard Kepa Arrizabalaga.

Mendy was a revelation with the Premier League club, and he culminated his debut season by winning the UEFA Champions League as the Blues defeated fellow Premier League club Manchester City in the final. Mendy thus became the first African goalkeeper to play in the Champions League final since Zimbabwean Bruce Grobbelaar for Liverpool in 1985. Confident in his own ability thanks to his support network, and with impressive efficiency on the line and feline flexibility, he also shows beautiful ease in the aerial game, a skill he showed during three years at Chelsea before moving to Al-Ahli in Saudi Arabia.

DID YOU KNOW?

A cousin to Édouard Mendy, the left-sided Real Madrid and former Olympique Lyonnais defender Ferland Mendy chose to tie his colours to the national team of France. The two men have no connection of kinship with Benjamin Mendy, the former player for Marseille and France. Both were annoyed to have been confused in certain shots published in the English tabloids with Benjamin during his well-publicised court cases.

FRANCE

Ferland
MENDY

BORN: 8 June 1995
Meulan-en-Yvelines,
France

HEIGHT: 1.80 m

POSITION: Defender

PROFESSIONAL CAREER:
Le Havre AC,
Olympique Lyonnais,
Real Madrid CF

I n the Mendy football family there are Bernard, Benjamin, Édouard, Étienne and all the others who walked the grass and graced the stadiums of Ligue 1, but none of them put down their boots at Real Madrid. Until, that is, Ferland Mendy. Having established himself in the crisp white shirt of the Spanish giants, Ferland can arguably state that he has had the most successful career of them all. His back story is quite a beautiful one.

A move from Le Havre to the mythical club trained by Zinedine Zidane via Lyon in less than two seasons. Has anyone done it better? In record time, Ferland has progressed from Ligue 2, Ligue 1, Olympique Lyonnais and the French national team and is now in the most revered dressing room in the world: a very real dream that has come true. However, if his story was a film it would not be one of a spoiled child.

A chaotic journey sprinkled with discipline problems: Mendy had to work for his success. Passing through the youth formation of Paris Saint-Germain between 2005 and 2012, his career appeared in jeopardy when at the age of 15 he found himself in a wheelchair. Arthritis of the hip, contracted at just 14, saw him leave PSG and his future football career was in doubt.

'For three months I was in the Necker hospital, in plaster,' Ferland recalled. 'The doctors told me that football was over for me; they even spoke to me of amputation.' Fortunately for Ferland and football lovers the world over, he recovered and continued to impress. As a player he hustled and as a man he is humble, well spoken and a great communicator.

The generation he is from is golden: Presnel Kimpembe, Kingsley Coman, Adrien Rabiot, Moussa Dembélé and Ferland Mendy all on the same card. His personality stood out early, as he is never short of jokes and pranks on his mates – behaviour that can perhaps be explained by the disappearance of the father figure. His dad's death was a tipping point that Ferland never speaks about and still today it's impossible to break through the armour. He locks this part of his life well away.

The Norman air of Le Havre gave him his first break, with three seasons and around 50 matches in Ligue 2. He was named as the best left back of the championship. These performances kindled interest elsewhere, and Lyon came calling in 2017. Not seen as a potential starter when joining, he soon confirmed himself as the best left back at the club and before long was living the dream at Real.

DID YOU KNOW?

Before being called by Didier Deschamps to the French team, the Real Madrid defender Ferland Mendy had never been selected with the French youth teams. His serious hip injury when he was in pre-training at Paris Saint-Germain almost forced him to quit football. He discovered the Château de Clairefontaine only when he was selected for the senior national team in 2018.

Lionel

MESSI

BORN: 24 June 1987
Rosario, Argentina

HEIGHT: 1.70 m

POSITION: Forward

PROFESSIONAL CAREER:
FC Barcelona,
Paris Saint-Germain FC,
Inter Miami CF

A glorious day in Qatar cemented a legacy. Argentina fulfilled the dream of a player who has graced the stadiums of the world with his sheer brilliance, hoisting the golden trophy that confirmed La Albiceleste as champions of the world. In the eyes of many Lionel Messi was the greatest of all time. The win over France, a penalty shoot-out success after a 3–3 draw in which Messi had struck twice, finally put paid to the suggestions that the diminutive superstar was unable to impose himself in his national team's colours.

The critics had a point up to then. After Argentina had been ousted from the 2018 tournament in Russia by the same French selection, losing by the odd goal in a seven-goal thriller, Messi announced his international retirement. Fortunately for football lovers around the globe, after a few months of abstinence the prodigy returned in March 2019. His comeback match ended in a 1–3 loss to Venezuela in Madrid, but it would of course get better!

The World Cup glory added to the earlier Copa América triumph of 2021, Argentina defeating Brazil 1–0 in the final in their great rival's own backyard. It was Messi's first international success at the fifth attempt and it was followed by a triumph in the Finalissima, a 3–0 defeat of European champions Italy at Wembley Stadium. Messi played a major part with a brace of assists.

Despite serious concerns about his growth in his adolescence, the young Argentinian was well nurtured by FC Barcelona at their iconic La Masia, the renowned training centre. Catalan educators loved the young boy who had landed in their midst like a gift from the South American gods. The kid from Rosario in northern Argentina was already the darling of his local club of Newell's Old Boys. The Catalan doctors imposed a heavy treatment based on hormone injections so the undersized Messi would not be handicapped by his stature.

At just 17 years of age and having forged an athletic body, Leo Messi discovered La Liga with the great Barça, making a debut in 2004 that marked the beginning of a story embroidered in golden letters. The immortal Argentinean exploded onto the scene with the Blaugrana and began a trophy haul that saw him claim seven Ballon d'Or awards. His time at Camp Nou ended in a tearful media conference in 2021 as he moved to PSG where, it's fair to say, his star was undimmed despite not always winning over the supporters. He latterly switched to MLS in the USA and signed for Inter Miami to write a whole new chapter.

MESSI

DID YOU KNOW?

A quintuplet and two assists in a 16–0 victory meant Messi was on fire in the shirt of Barcelona as he racked up these impressive numbers. However, it was not Lionel but his son Thiago, who at just six years of age was following in the footsteps of his father. With his youth team at La Masia, Messi Junior shone on the pitch but also had a critical eye. 'He likes to look at me, ask me questions and, when things are bad, he gives me grades,' dad Leo laughed.

ENGLAND

Mason
MOUNT

BORN: 10 January 1999
Portsmouth, England

HEIGHT: 1.81 m

POSITION: Midfielder

PROFESSIONAL CAREER:
Chelsea FC, SBV Vitesse,
Derby County FC,
Manchester United

The Italian coaches could not see what was right in front of their eyes: both Maurizio Sarri and Antonio Conte, who succeeded each other at the head of Chelsea between 2016 and 2019, did not believe in Mason Mount. Therefore, the Blues's own 'Pompey Boy', a nickname given because he had been born in the English seaside town of Portsmouth, had to travel to make his mark. At the age of 18 the English prodigy had the guts and desire to succeed far from home and immediately shone in the Dutch Eredivisie.

A loan spell at Vitesse Arnhem saw the league revel in the tremendous potential of the uninhibited Mount. An incessant presser of the ball coupled with a rare intelligence when in possession ensured that Mason Mount was never thrown off balance whomever he came up against. His coach at that time, Marc van Hintum, insisted that he was a brilliant talent. His dribbling skills and ability to eliminate opponents one on one complemented an already impressive picture.

At the end of the season in the Netherlands the two local giants Ajax and PSV Eindhoven had eyes firmly set on the rare pearl. Eventually, though, he returned home, but not immediately within the elite. The phenomenon landed at Derby and found a certain Frank Lampard there on the bench in his early managerial days. From the following season and appointed head of the Blues, the former Chelsea midfielder brought Mount home with him.

Passionate about football from childhood but frail, the young Mount joined the Boarhunt FC team, a club that by chance was a local Chelsea academy! A real football fanatic, Mason breathed football and his loved ones were convinced their protégé would make a breakthrough at the high level. From the age of six he went to the capital and joined the Chelsea training academy, but his father Tony still hesitated: the big London club had a reputation for giving pride of place to the stars and neglecting its own youth development.

'I explained to Mason that, since John Terry Chelsea had not integrated any youngsters into their professional ranks,' Tony said. Mason replied with confidence that he would be next! Having become a starter, Mount reached his peaks early to the point of competing in the final of the Champions League at just 22 years of age. In the summer of 2023 Manchester United splashed the cash on his potential, taking the England midfielder to Old Trafford.

MOUNT

Manuel

NEUER

BORN: 27 March 1986
Gelsenkirchen, Germany

HEIGHT: 1.93 m

POSITION: Goalkeeper

PROFESSIONAL CAREER:
FC Schalke 04,
Bayern Munich

The kid felt his wings growing. In the middle of a match it wasn't rare for young Manuel Neuer to abandon his own penalty area and go on the attack. His father Peter confirmed it, remembering of his 10-year-old son: 'Manuel loved his position as goalkeeper, but he wanted so much to participate in the game!'

Despite a certain technical ease, at the time the teenager was in the crosshairs of his trainers. In the youth categories at Schalke 04 and despite excellent performances and attendance at training, the judgement was that he was too frail. It took the intervention of Lothar Matuschak, one of the best coaches across the Rhine, and the Schalke 04 management to save young Neuer's place at the training centre. Matuschak was convinced that young Manuel was exceptional and had a football brain to go along with the physical presence.

The following year after a late growth spurt, the budding goalkeeper shot up a huge 20 cm and his body thickened, and he now measures 1.93 m and 92 kg. 'He became imposing in his goal,' one of his coaches, Bodo Menze, remembered, 'but Manuel also had very fluid, coordinated movements, like those of a ballet dancer.' His technical audacity also offered solutions to his team.

He was considered to be a first attacker thanks to his eye and his precision passing with his feet and know-how to initiate actions. As a youth 'BeckenNeuer' turned pro at Schalke, and within a few months he was installed in place of incumbent goalkeeper Frank Rost. In the spring of 2011 a choice needed to be made: the proposal of a contract from Bayern Munich had landed on the table of the Neuer family. It provided strength of roots and love of the jersey against ambition and the promise of a shot at all the main prizes.

Neuer, the former ultra of the Nordkurve of the Veltins-Arena, finally gave in to the Bavarian siren call. Glory and titles were within reach, not just with the Roten but also in the jersey of former world champion Germany in Brazil. Neuer manned the goal as the Germans won the tournament with a 1–0 win over Argentina in the final in Rio. It was a great comeback for the keeper, who had been plagued with injuries that kept him off the field for several months, including an operation on his foot.

DID YOU KNOW?

Young Afghan, Iraqi or Syrian refugees sometimes come across their idol. In 2014 Manuel Neuer created the Manuel Neuer Kids Foundation in the Buer district in Gelsenkirchen, a sociocultural structure that accommodates 100 children from troubled families. Despite his privileged status, the goalkeeper of the Nationalmannschaft has not forgotten his proletarian origins in a Ruhr in full deindustrialisation, the very place where he grew up.

BRAZIL

NEYMAR

BORN: 5 February 1992
Mogi das Cruzes, Brazil

HEIGHT: 1.75 m

POSITION: Forward

PROFESSIONAL CAREER:
Santos FC, FC Barcelona,
Paris Saint-Germain FC,
Al Hilal SFC

There is a Brazilian saying that 'Lightning never strikes twice in the same place, but in Santos she fell three times: for Pelé, for Robinho and for Neymar.' Very soon, all of Brazil had heard about this new genius of national football. Neymar asserted himself at the age of 17 as the new king of Brazilian football.

With the historic club of Pelé he collected titles in spades, including in 2011 a Copa Libertadores, but unlike King Pelé the Neymar clan did not resist the call of the big European clubs. Barça won the race for him, with an official bid of €57 million. In his first clásico against Real Madrid the new number 11 opened the scoring for a 2–1 victory for Barça.

Neymar stacked up the trophies in Catalonia, a sign of his talent being the *remontada* (comeback) that was fatal to PSG in the Champions League. Paris then decided to break the bank for the talented Brazilian, capturing him for an eye-watering €222 million. Neymar, in the shadow of Lionel Messi at Barcelona, arrived at Paris Saint-Germain as a rock star. Greeted at the Parc des Princes like the Messiah, he graced Ligue 1 with his class and even took over the penalty duties from Uruguayan goal machine Edinson Cavani.

Neymar bagged a domestic treble in his first season at the club, scoring 28 times in 30 matches, the first clutch of a swathe of prizes and goals at the Parisian giants. As much as the owners were happy with their continuous sweeping of the board locally, success in Europe was their driving ambition. With Neymar teaming up with young sensation Kylian Mbappé, hope sprung eternal.

On the international stage Neymar made his debut in 2010 in a fixture against the United States in New Jersey, but it was the World Cup in 2014 that was supposed to be his coronation. An untimely back injury, suffered in the quarter-final match against Colombia when he was caught by a knee from Juan Camilo Zúñiga, kept him out of the semi-final and he was forced to watch on as his team was humiliated in front of their adoring public by Germany 7–1.

His time at PSG often flattered to deceive, and he moved to Al Hilal in August 2023. The transfer fee was reported to be worth €90 million, making him the most expensive purchase in the Saudi Pro League.

DID YOU KNOW?

As an ultrasound was too expensive for the Neymar family, his parents didn't know the sex of their son until the day of his birth. His mum's favourite name was Mateus, but the family was hesitant. For a week Baby Neymar remained without a first name, until the day his dad, Neymar Senior, decided to declare his birth. With his wife they opted for Mateus, but on the way his father changed his mind and called him Neymar Junior. Thus, Neymar was born!

NEYMAR

Christopher
NKUNKU

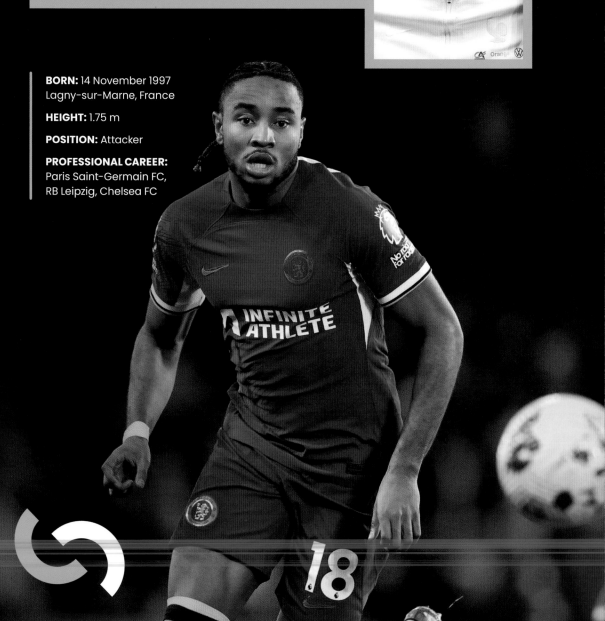

BORN: 14 November 1997
Lagny-sur-Marne, France

HEIGHT: 1.75 m

POSITION: Attacker

PROFESSIONAL CAREER:
Paris Saint-Germain FC,
RB Leipzig, Chelsea FC

The common point between Nicolas Anelka, Kingsley Coman, Moussa Diaby and Christopher Nkunku? They all play in an offensive position but are able to play elsewhere if required, and at different times they all went to seek their happiness far from their training club. Does PSG have a problem with its young people? Seemingly unable to keep their best youth or to offer them serious playing time at the club, the wisp of RB Leipzig is no exception.

After playing just 55 matches in five seasons Nkunku took his talents to the Bundesliga, where he became a star of the German championship, a French international and someone who was linked with a rumoured return to his former stomping ground. Everyone who has ever met Nkunku is unanimous: he feels football and does not shy away from the task at hand.

It is true that the small lad from Lagny-sur-Marne was not an obvious addition to the heavyweight court of European attackers. From his early days as a youngster he was smaller than his friends and certainly frailer. Thus he saw himself obliged by nature to become a different player, limiting his touches of the ball to the strict minimum and condemned to avoid the physical duels but able to read the game faster than other players on the field. He then naturally developed his own qualities of speed, stamina, technical qualities and a fierce shot.

Nkunku arrived at PSG in 2010 and was built up by also playing at the INF Clairefontaine academy before logically integrating into the youth section of the Parisian club. In his early stages he nevertheless had to be protected by his trainers for fear of seeing him break in two, such was his slight physique.

Young and talented, it appeared as though Nkunku had a bright future ahead of him in Paris, but the Parisian competition crushed everything in its passage. After beefing up his game and in Germany and on the European scene, Nkunku was named best player of the Bundesliga in the spring of 2022. It was deserved recognition in front of the stars of Bayern Munich and one more argument towards him becoming essential within the band in France's blue jersey under Didier Deschamps.

Nkunku was called up to the senior French squad for the first time for friendly matches against Ivory Coast and South Africa in March 2022, and he secured a mega-money move to Chelsea in the English Premier League in time for the start of the 2023–24 season.

DID YOU KNOW?

Unlike the younger generation, who are fans of Lionel Messi and Cristiano Ronaldo, Christopher Nkunku is rather admiring of another style. For a long time the Brazilian Willian was his favourite player. The profile of the former international was closer to his: a modest size, lively, technical and an outstanding passer. During the summer of 2015, invited by Laurent Blanc to participate in the preparation of the Parisian club in the United States, the kid fulfilled his dream: to meet his idol.

NIGERIA

Victor
OSIMHEN

BORN: 29 December 1998
Lagos, Nigeria

HEIGHT: 1.85 m

POSITION: Striker

PROFESSIONAL CAREER:
VfL Wolfsburg,
Royal Charleroi SC,
Lille OSC,
SSC Napoli

I n autumn 2015 the elite of European football recruiters arranged to meet in Chile, where for a month the best juniors from around the world were to compete in the U-17 FIFA World Cup. During the tournament one player stood out. Victor Osimhen played all seven matches for the Golden Eaglets, reaching the final and showing the watching crowd what he could offer by scoring at least one goal in each game up until the showpiece conclusion. In the quarter final he led Brazil on a merry dance, left them groggy and dazed in a 3–0 victory. Not surprisingly, he netted in the all-African final the opening goal in a 2–0 win over Mali on the way to ending the competition as the Golden Boot winner with 10 goals.

The young striker from the Ultimate Strikers Academy was suddenly in the sights of some renowned teams. In January 2016 it was finally the German club VfL Wolfsburg that showed itself the most persuasive, and Victor James Osimhen arrived among the Wolves of Lower Saxony – although it took a year to finalise the deal. His beginnings were timid in the Bundesliga: between physical glitches and severe competition from Mario Gómez, Divock Origi and Bas Dost, the frail striker hardly played with the Greens across the Rhine and remained an unfulfilled talent. Loaned in the summer of 2018 to Sporting Charleroi, Osimhen found his feet and explosiveness and scored 12 times in 25 appearances.

During the following off-season, buoyed by his success over the border, LOSC recalled their man and he enjoyed a successful season among the Mastiffs. He immediately took apart two giants of the French game, scoring sumptuous doubles against both Nantes and Saint-Étienne. During this time he also made his debut in the UEFA Champions League. Unfortunately, the COVID-19 pandemic in the spring of 2020 curtailed Lille's championship push and Osimhen's progress, although in the truncated campaign he still managed to finish level at the top of the scoring charts with Neymar at PSG, on 13 goals each.

Purchased for €12 million, Lille sold their talented asset for six times the fee, a club-record fee of €70 million and potentially rising to €80 million with add-ons, making him the most expensive African transfer to date. It was a nice financial transaction for the French club. Osimhen settled quickly into Serie A and soon became the darling of the Diego Armando Maradona Stadium, helping Napoli to the Scudetto.

OSIMHEN

DID YOU KNOW?

During the visit of FC Nantes to Pierre-Mauroy on 11 August 2019, Victor Osimhen was preparing to strike hard in his first match in the LOSC jersey. The Nigerian striker has not forgotten a funny episode from before the match: 'When leaving the bus, José Fonte told me: "If you score two goals, I'll take you to a restaurant." I replied: "Okay, captain!" He gave me an assist on the first goal, Nantes equalised, then I scored the winning goal. It was such an adrenaline shot.' For his part, the Portuguese was forced to book the table.

SPAIN

PEDRI

BORN: 25 November 2002
Bajamar, Spain

HEIGHT: 1.74 m

POSITION: Midfielder

PROFESSIONAL CAREER:
UD Las Palmas,
FC Barcelona

This is the last little marvel of Spanish football! Pedro González López, aka Pedri, does not at first glance look like much. An introverted presence, he becomes formidable as soon as he enters a football pitch and teases the ball. After growing up in the Canary Islands, his native archipelago, the pocket magician first succeeded with the club of his village, UD Tegueste.

At just 15 years of age he joined the flagship team of Las Palmas. His rise was dazzling since it only took a few weeks to secure a professional contract there, and aged 16 years, 9 months and 25 days Pedri became the youngest scorer with the club. His progress might have been thwarted in February 2018 when the Canarian teenager completed a trial at Real Madrid that ultimately proved inconclusive.

Pumped up and back in Las Palmas, Pedri gave it his all in the Segunda Division while boosting the attacking style of his team. Whether in the long game, in small spaces or diagonal passes, Pedri knew how to do everything. Of great precision in his passing and endowed with an incomparable vision of the game, the Spanish elf amazed his coaches. 'Pedri has the quality of making things easier around him and seeing the game before others,' Pepe Mel commented.

With his devastating hooks, small stature and refined style, the Iberian Harry Potter was a star standout. By recruiting Pedri, Barça did not hide that the jewel of Tegueste inevitably recalled with his technical ease a certain Iniesta on his arrival at the Blaugrana training base. In October 2020 Pedri played his first classico, and even if Real Madrid came out on top winning 3–1 the impish maestro played up to the occasion and delivered some early examples of his burgeoning talent.

For the national team his progress was just as swift. He celebrated his first cap in March 2021 against Greece in a match that ended in a 1–1 draw, and three months later he became one of the revelations of the European Championships, a tournament that saw La Roja reach the semi-finals. After a gruelling first season – Pedri even played at the Tokyo Olympics – and despite a thigh injury that kept him out for a spell, away from the field the little genius signed an extension of his contract with Barça in October 2021 that tied him to the club until 2026. The exit clause was then set by the Catalan club at . . . €1 billion!

DID YOU KNOW?

In October 2020 during a UEFA Champions League match against the Hungarians of Ferencvárosi, which FC Barcelona won 5–1 at Camp Nou, Pedri scored his very first goal in the Barça jersey. Previously, Ansu Fati had also found the net.
This was the first time in the history of the Catalan club that two players under the age of 18 had scored in the same European match.

ENGLAND

Jordan

PICKFORD

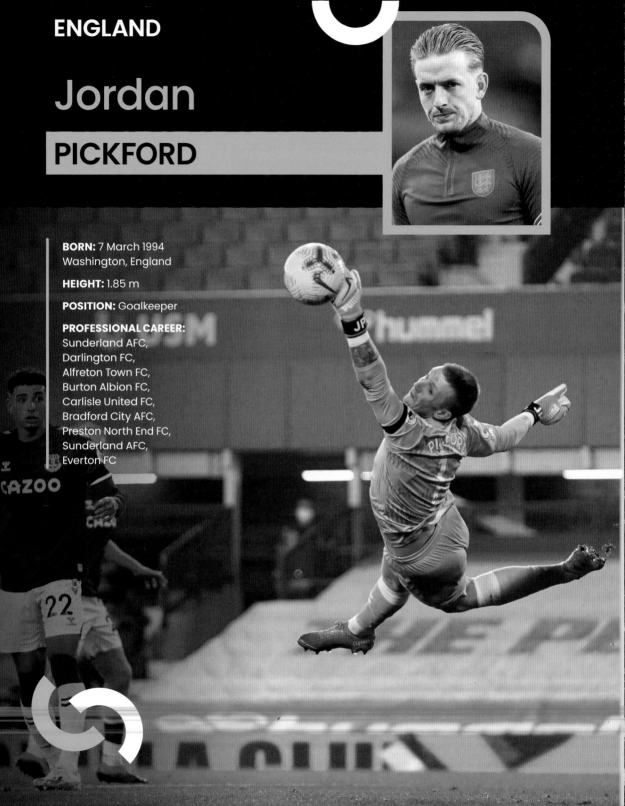

BORN: 7 March 1994
Washington, England

HEIGHT: 1.85 m

POSITION: Goalkeeper

PROFESSIONAL CAREER:
Sunderland AFC,
Darlington FC,
Alfreton Town FC,
Burton Albion FC,
Carlisle United FC,
Bradford City AFC,
Preston North End FC,
Sunderland AFC,
Everton FC

When Jordan Pickford parried a penalty from Colombian Carlos Bacca in the Round of 16 of the World Cup 2018 in Moscow, he ended the curse. The hero of the Three Lions had ensured that England won a penalty shoot-out and squeezed through the door into the quarter finals. They progressed to the semi-finals, the first time they had travelled that far since Italia in 1990.

It was the Everton goalkeeper, with just three caps to his name, who erased the memory of a succession of custodians who were unable to emerge from the shadows of their illustrious predecessors, world-class talents who patrolled between the posts such as Gordon Banks, Ray Clemence and Peter Shilton. Not bad for a 24-year-old boy with great maturity who never shirked responsibility. 'Nothing scares me,' Pickford admitted. 'Critics don't affect me; they can only make me better.'

Some observers spoke of arrogance, while others defended this very mobile goalkeeper with an exceptional left foot. His counterpart at Everton, the Dutchman Maarten Stekelenburg, pushed onto the bench by the little genius, willingly admitted it: 'Jordan knows what he is worth; he has great self-confidence,' he said. 'He works a lot and, above all, never panics. Nothing can fluster him.'

This appeared to be a logical continuation of a chaotic start to the journey to the top, a journey that saw six loans from Jordan's club Sunderland to Darlington, Alfreton Town, Burton Albion, Carlisle United, Bradford City and Preston North End, clubs spread throughout the lower divisions of British football. From the Conference Premier to the championship, the kid from Sunderland had to grit his teeth to satisfy his passion.

When 'Speedy' walked onto his first pitches he was placed in the goal because he was the biggest of the band, and his brother Richard encouraged him to stay in goal. In an irony of fate his size was talked about 16 years later, during the World Cup. In the first round England cracked in front of the Belgian sharpshooters 0–1, and on the goal scored by the Red Devil Adnan Januzaj, Jordan Pickford seemed too short. He shook that off and now stands tall as an English giant.

DID YOU KNOW?

The Merseyside derby between Liverpool and Everton makes him nervous. Two episodes have already marked the career of Jordan Pickford against the Reds. In December 2018 at Anfield Jordan was caught out by an innocuous ball, and in the 96th minute he was beaten at close range by Divock Origi. The one-goal defeat was cruel for the Toffees. Almost two years later, this time at Goodison Park, Jordan's kamikaze outing caught Liverpool defender Virgil van Dijk and injured his right knee. Pickford escaped a red card as the Dutch defender was offside.

SPAIN

Sergio
RAMOS

BORN: 30 March 1986
Camas, Spain

HEIGHT: 1.84 m

POSITION: Defender

PROFESSIONAL CAREER:
Sevilla FC, Sevilla Atlético,
Real Madrid,
Paris Saint-Germain FC,
Sevilla FC

Impermeable to pressure, Sergio Ramos is a boon for a coach but a nightmare for opposing attackers. In his role as a leader in the locker room, the Andalusian defender is a model captain whose voice carries weight and impresses any player as they prepare to enter the stadium. His coach at Real Madrid, Zinedine Zidane, said of him that the boy was noble in the sense of fidelity and game design and that his trust in him was limitless and without fault.

A teammate of 'Zizou' during his last season on a field, in 2005–06, the Madrid 'Terminator' is the perfect relay for the authority of the Marseillais on the pitch. Inevitably, Ramos's detractors often have a field day because he is never indifferent to any fixture and his conception of duty is pushed to the extreme.

If it is necessary to intimidate competitors Ramos does not lack ideas. The 20 expulsions during his career started as soon as he came of age in the jersey of Sevilla FC. 'Sometimes I get shot down. Sometimes I get praised. And, here, everyone will say that I am the saviour because I scored,' the Spaniard commented in March 2017 after a 3–1 success for Real at Napoli. 'Nothing like that! I'm just doing my job.'

Despite this false modesty, 'Churu' – so nicknamed by Javier Saviola – became a legend with the Merengues in becoming the hero of La Decima. In the 2014 Champions League final in Lisbon, Ramos equalised in additional time against Atlético de Madrid with a thumping header before Real eased to success in extra time, coming out on top 4–1. This was how the White House, to which he is so attached, won the 10th Champions League crown in its glorious history.

Less flashy four years later was the condemnation Ramos received in some quarters for his coming together with Liverpool forward Mohamed Salah. The Egyptian was forced to leave the pitch in the Champions League final with a dislocated shoulder. Ramos's love of bullfighting never stood out as well as it did that day in Kyiv. The person who sums it up best remains one of his first trainers, Joaquin Caparrós, in Seville: 'Sergio was hungry, he loved competition,' he said. 'It is this temperament that made it possible to succeed.'

After more than 450 matches for Real and winning everything that could possibly be won, Ramos made the switch to Paris and a link-up with Messi and co at PSG in 2021–22 before a swift return to Spain with Sevilla for 2023–24.

Marcus

RASHFORD

BORN: 31 October 1997
Manchester, England

HEIGHT: 1.80 m

POSITION: Forward

PROFESSIONAL CAREER:
Manchester United FC

A pure-bred Mancunian, the young Marcus Rashford could easily have grown up at the Sky Blues but City training officials found him too weak. Taken to football matches from the age of six by older brother Dwain, the youngest Rashford discovered how fun the game was at the Fletcher Moss Rangers. Three years later Manchester United opened its doors and the kid from Wythenshawe, a popular area of Greater Manchester, flourished there until his adolescence.

Despite many clubs in the United Kingdom trying to lure him Marcus remained loyal to the Red Devils, and in the youth categories he accomplished amazing feats thanks in particular to a keen sense of goal. Outside the playing arena he came across as lacking assurance. His youthful features and monotonous tone when he answered media questions did not at first sight give him a sense of his own ability. That was to change as he grew and became a major voice for social change in his homeland.

In early 2016, taking advantage of an avalanche of injuries up front, the English teenager was called into the first-team squad by Louis van Gaal for a debut in the Europa League against the Danes of FC Midtjylland. The slender striker was thrown into the Theatre of Dreams and scored a brace in a 5–1 victory. Aged 18 years and 117 days in his first professional outing, he became Manchester United's youngest goal scorer in European competition. He followed that up by netting a brace in his Premier League debut against Arsenal and scored the winner in his first Manchester derby. Perfect achievements to enable him to enter the hearts of supporters.

Before the European Championships in France he was called up to the England team as a potential partner to Harry Kane. After just three minutes of play during a warm-up match against Australia he slammed home his first goal in the shirt of the Three Lions. As with his catches of the ball, the apprentice champion is obviously a boy in a hurry. Despite his size he impresses with his balance and sturdiness. Everyone appreciates his fluidity around the attack, his astonishing finesse in the pass or the sheer power of his shooting. Excellent at hitting a clean strike on the run, Rashford made it one of his specialties.

He even made dead balls a part of his repertoire, scoring a glorious free kick against Wales at the 2022 FIFA World Cup in Qatar – one of three goals he scored during that tournament.

DID YOU KNOW?

In his very first league appearance at Old Trafford in February 2016, Marcus Rashford scored his first Premier League goal against Arsenal, a 3–2 win with a double to his credit. After these exploits the journalists rushed to talk to the new hero. To a reporter who asked him how he intended to celebrate the feat the young Red Devils forward, just 18 years old, answered full of confidence: 'I'm not going to celebrate anything. I have a chemistry test tomorrow!'

Antonee

ROBINSON

BORN: 8 August 1997
Milton Keynes, England

HEIGHT: 1.83 m

POSITION: Defender

PROFESSIONAL CAREER:
Everton FC,
Bolton Wanderers FC,
Wigan Athletic FC,
Fulham FC

Antonee Robinson is an athletic attacking fullback who shot to stardom off the back of Fulham's most recent promotion to the English Premier League (EPL). Although Robinson was born in England he is a full United States international, having qualified through a father who grew up in New York and played collegiate soccer at Duke University. He is also of Jamaican descent through his paternal grandmother.

Robinson is a product of the Everton academy, but injuries hampered his early career and he made his competitive league debut in the Championship with Bolton Wanderers, for whom he was a regular starter in 2017–18. He had a further year in England's second tier on loan at Wigan, where his impressive displays prompted the Latics to make the deal permanent. Robinson took his performances to a new level in 2019–20 and was a star performer in the Wigan team that embarked on a run of 10 clean sheets from 11 games in the latter stages of the campaign.

Robinson's career progression was almost derailed by a heart problem. He was set to move from Wigan to AC Milan on the January 2020 transfer deadline day but the move fell through due to a heart irregularity that was discovered in his medical exam. He moved to Fulham for the new season but the London club was unable to avoid relegation from the top tier. No matter: a stellar Championship campaign in 2021–22 underpinned by no fewer than 36 appearances from their rock-solid left back saw the club win the title and promotion. Robinson's form earned him a place in the EFL Team of the Year.

Propelled back into the EPL, both Fulham and Robinson went from strength to strength. His club form ensured he was a fixture for the United States men's national soccer team during qualifications for the 2022 World Cup and again in Qatar. He became an internet sensation following the United States's victory over Iran and progression to the knock-out stage of the tournament. Images and footage of Robinson comforting the Iran players quickly went viral on social media, where he won praise for his empathy.

Off the field Robinson is a talented piano player and a proponent of card tricks and can solve the Rubik's cube in record time. He often does a back flip to celebrate scoring a goal.

DID YOU KNOW?

Robinson's nickname, 'Jedi', stems from his childhood. In fact, he earned the nickname as a five year old as a consequence of his passion for the *Star Wars* franchise. 'I feel weird being called Antonee,' Robinson told ESPN. 'I prefer being called Jedi.'

RODRI

BORN: 22 June 1996
Madrid, Spain

HEIGHT: 1.9 m

POSITION: Defensive
midfielder

PROFESSIONAL CAREER:
Villarreal CF,
Atlético de Madrid,
Manchester City FC

With a stroke of genius, Rodri delivered for an entire group and thus ensured the supreme coronation. The date 10 June 2023 will live long in football history, in particular the 68th minute of the UEFA Champions League final in Istanbul. After Manuel Akanji created an opening, Bernardo Silva managed to get to the byline. Inter Milan repelled the initial movement, but there was a major problem for the Nerazzurri: the ball found its way to Spanish maestro Rodri. We know the quality of the strike that followed from the Madrilenian of the Citizens who, from an instantaneous attempt, beautifully lodged the ball under the crossbar of the goal, leaving the Internazionale goalkeeper André Onana with little chance.

In making the breakthrough and ensuring the final success of a 1–0 victory, Rodrigo Hernández Cascante offered the big-eared cup to fans of Manchester City and a Pep Guardiola-inspired team that can finally be placed alongside the coach's former success at FC Barcelona. As for Rodri his 2022–23 season, already staggering with the double of the FA Cup and Premier League already in hand, was far from finished. Eight days later in Rotterdam, Rodri was omnipotent in the midfield of La Roja as he helped blow away the Nations League hopes of Croatia by winning the final 0–0 after extra time and 5–4 on penalties.

Often compared with Sergio Busquets for his ability to function as a rotating midfield anchor, the versatile Rodri possesses more power than his glorious elder. All defenders and goalkeepers notably fear his striking of the ball, even those who have seen it all before. Able to cover the whole field, the Castilian does not often need the support of his teammates to carry out his job. Recovery, relaunch, perceptive passing and shooting, he always relishes his capital role in the heart of the game and plays with a maturity and tactical sense that place him above his peers in that position.

Rodri plays just as metronomically with both feet, at a volume and pace that is the envy of others. The boy experienced a meteoric rise to such an extent that his teammates rely on his constant ability to be the dynamo around which the team's attacking style is built. Despite his new status as a star of European football, the Hispanic international does not want to change anything. If Pep Guardiola can legitimately be proud of his group – and as the treble winners why wouldn't he be? – the Catalan Rodri certainly remains one of the technician's finest discoveries.

RODRI

PORTUGAL

Cristiano
RONALDO

BORN: 5 February 1985
Funchal, Portugal

HEIGHT: 1.87 m

POSITION: Forward

PROFESSIONAL CAREER:
Sporting CP,
Manchester United FC,
Real Madrid CF,
Juventus FC,
Manchester United FC,
Al Nassr FC

It's the feeling of summer. At the beginning of July 2018, the conversations of football lovers invariably turned around the transfer window. After nine seasons at Real Madrid and the third Champions League in a row won in the jersey of the Merengues, Cristiano Ronaldo announced his departure for Juventus. The Portuguese star admitted to having been stunned by the standing ovation of the Piedmontese public after his incredible goal from an overhead kick during the UEFA Champions League quarter final in the spring against the Bianconeri. For €100 million, 'CR7' was heading for Turin.

Everywhere he has been the champion has always electrified the crowds and Juventus was no different, Ronaldo bagging goals aplenty before making an emotional return to Manchester United, the scene of his breakthrough onto the global stage as a worldwide phenomenon. A hard worker with the physique of an athlete, Cristiano exudes football.

Technically, he is unquestionably the best. With Lionel Messi he formed a duo of extraterrestrials and, as per the Argentinean, the Lusitanian broke record after record on the stadiums of world football. The latest? The Madeiran became the first player to win – unheard of – a league title in the three biggest championships in Europe: the English Premier League, Spanish Liga and Italian Serie A.

From Alex Ferguson to Manchester United to Zinedine Zidane at Real Madrid, his coaches have always installed him in the best conditions for him to best express his tremendous talent. To top it off, while Portugal has so far only gleaned a few international accolades, the child of Funchal led the Seleção to the supreme title at Euro 2016. Injured at the start of the final against the French team Ronaldo left his partners but, limping on the edge of the field and inhabited by such a desire to win, he transmitted this passion for victory to the whole group.

In 2003, when he was just 18 years of age, his training club, Sporting CP, played a friendly match against Manchester United. The United players were so stunned by the qualities of the young man that they eventually convinced Sir Alex Ferguson to recruit this future genius. This was the start of an extraordinary career that saw him become the highest goal scorer in men's international football history. Unfortunately for his legacy, his second spell at Old Trafford ended in an acrimonious exit and with a move to Al Nassr in Saudi Arabia.

RONALDO

Arriving at the age of 12 in Lisbon, little Cristiano was expelled from his school after launching a chair at his teacher, who had made fun of the modest situation of his family and also of his accent. Born on the island of Madeira, despite tears of anger the boy was already showing a lot of character. Sports trainers quickly appreciated the kid's willingness to pull through the tough days.

Bukayo

SAKA

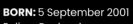

BORN: 5 September 2001
Ealing, England

HEIGHT: 1.78 m

POSITION: Right winger

PROFESSIONAL CAREER:
Arsenal FC

With his Brazilian appearance, the young Englishman precociously inherited a nickname that suited him perfectly: 'Sakinho'. With his swaying dribbles, the Gunners star excels at unseating an opposing defence and brings immediate danger in the final third. The fluidity of his gestures are amplified by a sharp technique, especially more impressive when the whole thing is done with speed and disconcerting execution.

Since his first excursion on the pitch with Watford, Saka has succeeded in everything he tried. He was only seven years old when he arrived at the Arsenal Academy Hale End, and his coaches were quickly convinced they had signed a star. A wonderful love story then began in the greater north London suburbs. Young Saka knows the notion of sacrifice, and in particular that he was not able to live like a normal teenager; in the Gunners training centre they do not mess around with the education of their future talents. While his football was inspired by local stars such as Thierry Henry, Dennis Bergkamp and Nwankwo Kanu, it was nevertheless a Swede who allowed him to take off. The youth coach at Arsenal, Fredrik Ljungberg, became the mentor for Saka, who was always listening and asking for advice.

In the 2019 off-season, while taking advantage of the absence in Arsenal's midfield of Aaron Ramsey and Alex Iwobi, the young winger was launched onto the big stage. Asked by the Nigerian Federation to link up with them, he declined the invitation of the Super Eagles and had only one objective: to shine with the English Three Lions. In October 2020 Saka was called by Gareth Southgate and earned his first cap in a friendly match against Wales at Wembley, a fixture that was won 3–0.

He returned to the temple of English football during Euro 2021 when England reached the final but, just like Marcus Rashford and Jadon Sancho, Bukayo Saka saw his penalty in the final shoot-out against Italy fail. Far from discouraging him, this ordeal reinforced the desire of the one Pierre-Emerick Aubameyang affectionately calls 'Little Chilli'. With confidence from coach at the Gunners Mikel Arteta, Bukayo Saka achieved a high standard during the 2022–23 season. Although Arsenal, long in the lead, was finally overtaken in the last straight by Manchester City in the title race, the hard-hitting Gunner had nothing to reproach himself for.

DID YOU KNOW?

Of Nigerian origin through his parents and from the Yoruba ethnic group, Saka owes his first name to his grandmother: *bukayo* literally means 'God has added joy to my life'. The Gunner explained that his grandmother was very keen on it: 'She wanted me to add happiness to the family, so she named me thus,' he revealed. His parents did not procrastinate for long before giving him this baptismal name.

SAKA

Mohamed

SALAH

BORN: 15 June 1992
Nagrig, Egypt

HEIGHT: 1.75 m

POSITION: Forward

PROFESSIONAL CAREER:
Al Mokawloon Al Arab SC,
FC Basel, Chelsea FC,
ACF Fiorentina, AS Roma,
Liverpool FC

No one has forgotten that loose shoulder. In Egypt there was the nose of Cleopatra at the time of the pharaohs, and more than 20 centuries later there is Mohamed Salah's collarbone. Injured in a manly clash with Sergio Ramos in the Champions League final between Real Madrid and Liverpool in May 2018, the Egyptian striker almost missed the World Cup in Russia. Especially cruel was that it was Salah who carried his team almost single-handedly through qualification.

After a race against time Mohamed Salah returned to the group and even scored twice in the global competition, but Egypt's elimination was confirmed. It was obviously in Europe that 'Mo' had become a twinkling star. This space devourer who combined speed and skills had all the qualities of a spectacular player. This was a long way to travel for the child of Basyoun forced to change buses five times to reach Cairo when he went as a teenager with the Arab Contractors. It was a test that forged his character.

Rejected in 2011 by Zamalek, in Switzerland and at FC Basel more precisely Mohamed revealed himself. A transfer to Chelsea followed two years later, but he failed to establish himself at the forefront of the Blues' attack and featured in just 13 games over a two and a half year period at Stamford Bridge.

It was better in Italian Serie A, where the Egyptian expanded his footballing spectrum. At Fiorentina and then at Roma Salah he developed his tactical sense and, above all, became a much more efficient finisher, an area in which he had been deficient for a long time. Able to score goals off dazzling counterattacks from his own half of the field, the 'Pharoah' shone in the Italian capital before making a move to Liverpool.

Reds' boss Jürgen Klopp immediately fell in love with his new signing. 'Even if he doesn't score he is very useful because he stretches the opposing defences,' Klopp said. 'It opens spaces for my other attackers.' He had the nerves for the big occasion, as his second-minute penalty in the 2019 UEFA Champions League final against Tottenham Hotspur showed. It was the fastest-ever goal in a Champions League showdown. When Salah takes action it's usually all of Anfield that takes up the chorus of his anthem, to the tune of 'Sit Down' by James. With such talent, there are rarely any false notes.

DID YOU KNOW?

In 2018 during the elections in Egypt, Mohamed Salah could have been the challenger of the-then head of state, General el-Sisi. Indeed, to challenge the absence of a real opposition some Egyptian voters chose to slip the name of the football star into the ballot box. The Reds striker finished second in the ballot . . . without showing up! At the foot of the pyramids Salah was able to appreciate his immense popularity.

Jadon

SANCHO

BORN: 25 March 2000
London, England

HEIGHT: 1.80 m

POSITION: Winger

PROFESSIONAL CAREER:
Borussia Dortmund,
Manchester United FC,
Borussia Dortmund (loan)

After Jadon Sancho's big season his performances earned him a score of 84 in the famous FIFA 20 video game, published by EA Sports. Surprised by this total, the player complained on social networks that he had not been better rewarded. Game controller in hand, Jadon Sancho was keen to improve his status. The English striker said he was particularly surprised to only have 77 on assists – according to a very personal estimate, he believed he deserved a rating of 90.

Like a gift from heaven, the young English winger runs with feints of the body. On his right side Jadon Sancho amazes observers with his liveliness, but that's not his only skill set. The kid from Camberwell has short and disarming changes of direction that are torture for defenders. Not surprisingly he was nicknamed 'The Rocket', as he excelled in the art of the opposite and the devastating gesture.

Such are his positive qualities it's easy to overlook the shortcomings in his defensive armoury and an almost non-existent heading game. That's not really his thing, but the prodigy who forged a unique style in his childhood by confusing his friends in endless football games played on the streets of the popular southern suburbs of London evolved by instinct. The street was his playground, and his competitiveness was such that he often went home in a sulk if he lost!

Brought up by parents from Trinidad and Tobago, Jadon Sancho trained at Watford before securing a big move to Manchester City. Pep Guardiola protected him until a complete misunderstanding led him to exile. Sancho was expecting an indication of more playing time in his contract and was subsequently annoyed when the Citizens left him out of their pre-season tour of the United States. Slighted and in a hurry to play, the gifted Londoner slammed the door on City.

He signed for Borussia Dortmund. Sancho's performances were sensational, goals and assists racked up by the bagful and star shows that had teams queueing up for his services. When he left City he had Arsenal, Tottenham, Bayern Munich and RB Leipzig all keen on him, but it was the Yellow Wall that benefited from his charms.

Inspired by his idol Ronaldinho, Jadon Sancho had the ability to attempt supernatural skills while still being effective. Supporting evidence can be seen during the 2018–19 season, when at just 18 years of age he became the Bundesliga's top assist provider. Launched into the big time by Lucien Favre, a talent scout, and well helped by Dortmund's attacking profile, Jadon Sancho, in line with Kylian Mbappé and Erling Braut Haaland, dazzled the crowds.

A switch back to Manchester and the red side to United saw him wow crowds once more.

GERMANY

Leroy
SANÉ

BORN: 11 January 1996
Essen, Germany

HEIGHT: 1.83 m

POSITION: Forward

PROFESSIONAL CAREER:
FC Schalke 04,
Manchester City FC,
FC Bayern Munich

SANÉ

What possessed German national team manager Joachim Löw to deprive himself of Leroy Sané for the World Cup in Russia in 2018? In his list, the one who had just been crowned champion of England with Manchester City and author of a rich season of Premier League exploits was conspicuous by his absence. To everyone's surprise 'Jogi' preferred Julian Brandt. Admittedly, the failure of Germany and their first-round elimination were not due just to the absence of the stirring kid from the Ruhr, but all the same his omittance was a surprise.

Already during Euro 2016 in France German supporters had complained about the lack of playing time granted to this great Ronaldinho fan. Thus, during the semi-final loss against France in Marseille at 0–2 the future Citizen had only come onto the field in the last quarter of an hour. However, a few weeks previously while in the jersey of Schalke 04 he had accomplished a mind-blowing performance against Real Madrid in the Champions League.

Elusive, the young winger had driven the Spanish defenders to distraction. During the second leg of the Round of 16 fixture the German club achieved an incredible result by winning 4–3 at the Santiago-Bernabéu Stadium. Too bad for Schalke and Leroy Sané, the Merengues won 2–0 in the first leg to oust the team from Gelsenkirchen.

Already experienced in European games at the age of 20, Sané continued his apprenticeship in the Champions League with Manchester City. His performances down the flank for the Citizens pleased his boss Pep Guardiola, even if Guardiola reproached him occasionally for his lack of consistent effort and a certain propensity to drift away from his assigned position.

An interesting aside saw Sané cost a punter a tidy sum in 2017. In a Champions League elimination tie against AS Monaco at the Etihad Stadium the German arrow netted the final goal in a 5–3 success and thus deprived the poor punter of a winning ticket. For €2 the punter in question had bet on City to win 4–3, and that goal cost a win of €34,200! Sané heard about the unfortunate incident and tweeted an apology. 'I read that in the newspapers . . . Sorry for the poor guy,' he posted after the match.

Sané made his national team debut in 2015 in a friendly against France and went on to reach a half century of caps at the 2022 FIFA World Cup in Qatar.

DID YOU KNOW?

Rare enough to be reported: already with a double Senegalese and German passport, Leroy Sané also has a French one thanks to his father Souleymane, a former striker in the Bundesliga who also holds French nationality. The son was named in honour of Claude Le Roy, a specialist in African football who coached his father in Dakar. 'I was born and raised in Germany,' Leroy said. 'I still have family in France, but I feel German.'

PORTUGAL

Bernardo

SILVA

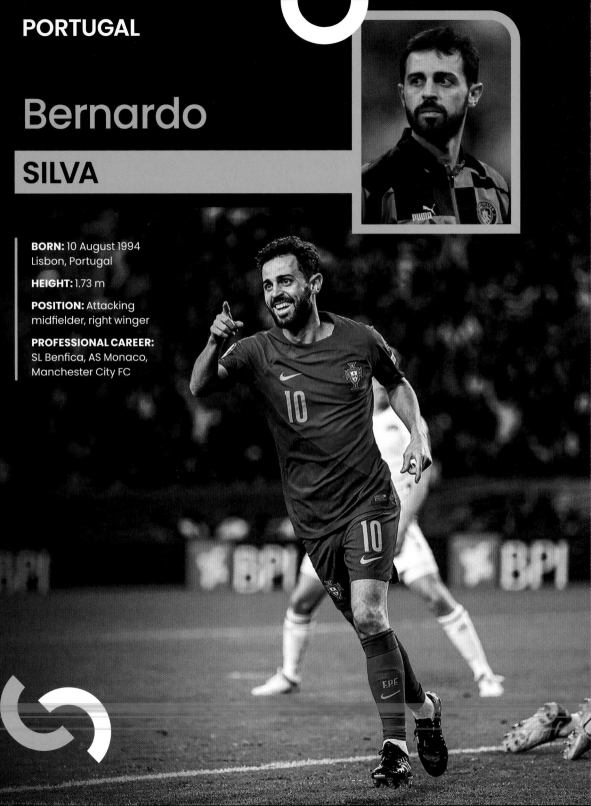

BORN: 10 August 1994
Lisbon, Portugal

HEIGHT: 1.73 m

POSITION: Attacking
midfielder, right winger

PROFESSIONAL CAREER:
SL Benfica, AS Monaco,
Manchester City FC

Heading for Seixal, where the Benfica training centre is located, youth coach Fernando Chalana equipped his protégé, none other than Bernardo Silva, with an evocative nickname: 'Messizinho' (little Messi). Of incredible vivacity and unequalled skill, the child nevertheless had difficulty standing out from the crowd in the initial stages. 'At this period of my life physique mattered a lot, and I was really very little,' the Portuguese will-o'-the-wisp recalled. At Benfica the standards were exceedingly high and they placed an emphasis on strength, meaning that despite everything the gateway to the first team remained stubbornly locked for Silva. 'I trained finally with the pro group but as a left back,' Silva said, 'so I understood that I had no future at Benfica.'

Then manager at the Lisbon Eagles Jorge Jesus just did not believe in his clever schemer, considering him too small to progress. 'He thinks faster than he is short,' Hélder Cristóvão, his B-team coach, assured. Only one option remained for this relentless person who, despite a lack of playing time, did not give up and secured a loan move to an ambitious club, joining up with AS Monaco in the 2014 off-season. He was barely at the Principality club before they exercised the right to purchase him from his parent team.

Leonardo Jardim felt it was the right move: 'Bernardo creates huge problems for an opposing defence thanks to his movement. He is also important in the transition phase as well as in the construction of our moves.' When the Portuguese schemer was deployed in an off-centre role to better fit into the system his elegant touches off the left foot were a feast for the eyes. Unpredictable in his choices, Bernardo Silva became an essential pawn of an AS Monaco team that stubbornly shook off the challenge of PSG and was crowned Champions of France in 2017.

Silva's guilty pleasure was holding on to possession, something that led to him being considered ripe for a bigger club. 'I often joked with him, saying that he was a player made for Barça,' João Tralhão, who also managed him at Benfica, recalled. It was not Barcelona but Pep Guardiola's Manchester City that stole him away from the south of France. He went on to land that historic treble in 2023, creating and scoring with abandon in a superb City set-up. It was a wonderful case of revenge for the frail toddler who has grown into the main man.

DID YOU KNOW?

On the evening of the elimination of the Champions League semi-final against Real Madrid in 2022, the Portuguese international admitted to a Madrid player his desire to play for Real: 'Tell Florentino to sign me; I want to play here!' Silva allegedly said. Bernardo loved the atmosphere at the Santiago Bernabéu and was potentially after a change of scenery. The following season the teams reconvened in the Champions League when Real again met City at the semi-final stage, and it was the star performance of the Portuguese that single-handedly eliminated the title holders!

SOUTH KOREA

Heung-min

SON

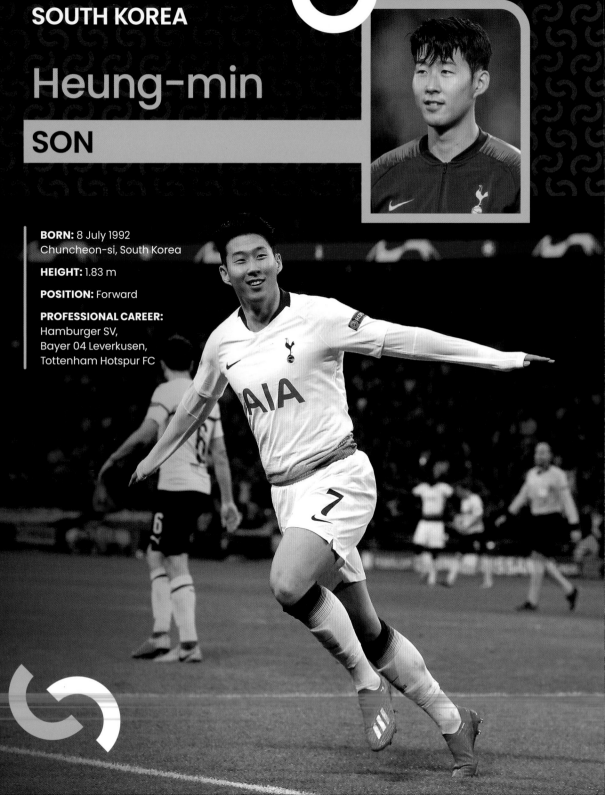

BORN: 8 July 1992
Chuncheon-si, South Korea

HEIGHT: 1.83 m

POSITION: Forward

PROFESSIONAL CAREER:
Hamburger SV,
Bayer 04 Leverkusen,
Tottenham Hotspur FC

To escape the obligations of military service in his country Son Heung-min found the right vein of form. In South Korea some champions are exempt from donning fatigues and carrying a rifle if they land medals of global importance, and during the summer of 2018 the Asian striker took up the challenge: that of participating with Korea's U-21 selection in the Asian games.

On Indonesian soil the champion forward led the young South Koreans to the final, during which they dominated Japan and claimed a 2–1 success in extra time. If placed it would have been a successful bet, and Son returned home with a winner's medal around his neck that saved him from the obstacle course, push-ups and guard towers!

From an early age the boy had always known how to adapt and discovered football in hardly encouraging circumstances. Punished by his father, the young Taeguk warrior was told to learn to tame a leather ball. Intoxicated by long minutes of juggling, the 10 year old learned the skills required to dominate that sphere. He was just a teenager barely out of his cocoon when he joined the Hamburg training centre. At a young age and thrust into a different culture, for young Son this was like living on a different planet.

'I didn't know anyone,' the dyed in the wool South Korean admitted. 'I thank all the great players for saying a word to me when I needed support. For example, Rafael van der Vaart and Ruud van Nistelrooy were helpful for me in Hamburg.' In the Bundesliga Son quickly became a phenomenon, and his express pace and determination to push his actions to the end seduced the media and spectators.

His debut in the Champions League drew a sizeable audience back home in his native country. 'At kick-off, it was five o'clock in the morning in Seoul and they were all up watching,' a visibly moved Son said. 'I felt like I owed them something, [that] it's my responsibility to play well.' Hence the diligent hours of training and the stubbornness to never let an opportunity pass him by. After a timid debut season at Tottenham, to whom he switched in 2015 from Bayer 04 Leverkusen, Son became better than a stand-in for Harry Kane. He instead created one of the great Premier League partnerships, the Son–Kane double act – a vital part of Tottenham's progression to the 2019 Champions League final.

SON

DID YOU KNOW?

On the football stock exchange he is among the most bankable assets in the game. The South Korean Son Heung-min has become one of the most expensive and valuable pieces on the chessboard of world football: his transfer in 2015 to Tottenham for €30 million was one of the highest fees paid for a player of Asian origin. At the age of 27 the forward some journalists nicknamed 'Sonaldo' for his sense of goal and explosiveness is a real star from Seoul.

AUSTRALIA

Harry
SOUTTAR

BORN: 22 October 1998
Aberdeen, Scotland

HEIGHT: 1.98 m

POSITION: Defender

PROFESSIONAL CAREER:
Dundee United FC,
Stoke City, Ross County FC,
Fleetwood Town FC,
Stoke City, Leicester City FC

On the rare occasions Harry Souttar visits Australia his height is not the only thing that stands out. Souttar's accent is not one usually associated with sunny Australia, and that's because he was born and raised half a world away in Scotland. He grew up in a village named Luthermuir with a Scottish father and a mother who was born in Western Australia, meaning he is eligible to play for both Scotland and Australia at international level.

While older brother John was capped by Scotland Harry never received such a call up, but he did come to the attention of more than one Australian working and playing in the UK as someone who could bolster the Socceroos squad. As a result, Socceroos coach Graham Arnold began to circle in 2019 to convince Souttar to switch allegiances.

After initially playing for Australia's U-23 side, Souttar was eventually called up by Arnold in 2019 for the nation's World Cup qualifiers. His debut came against Nepal in Canberra, when he scored two goals from corners in a 5–0 demolition job that showcased the towering defender's aerial prowess. There was no turning back . . .

Souttar became a fixture in the side that embarked on a run of 10 straight wins in qualifying – a record – but then in November 2021, during a qualifying match against Saudi Arabia, he suffered a severe ACL injury that ultimately ruled him out for the rest of qualifying and for almost a year for his club Stoke City.

Incredibly, Souttar's second game back from his knee injury was no less an occasion than Australia's opening match of the 2022 World Cup against France. He was rock solid in that affair, then he played a key role in Australia's next two games in Qatar: victories against Tunisia and Denmark in which the Socceroos kept a clean sheet. The Aussies then gave eventual champions Argentina a scare in a 2–1 loss in the Round of 16.

A month later it was announced Souttar would play in the English Premier League when Leicester City confirmed it had made the 24-year-old defender a deadline-day signing in a record transfer deal for an Australian. 'It's great news for Harry,' Socceroos coach Arnold explained, 'but also Australian football and the Socceroos, because I truly believe he will have the captain's armband on one day.'

DID YOU KNOW?

Harry Souttar had never even set foot in Australia before he was called in to the Socceroos squad during the early stages of qualification for the 2022 World Cup. Following the nation's greatest-ever World Cup showing, he's a national hero.

ENGLAND

Raheem

STERLING

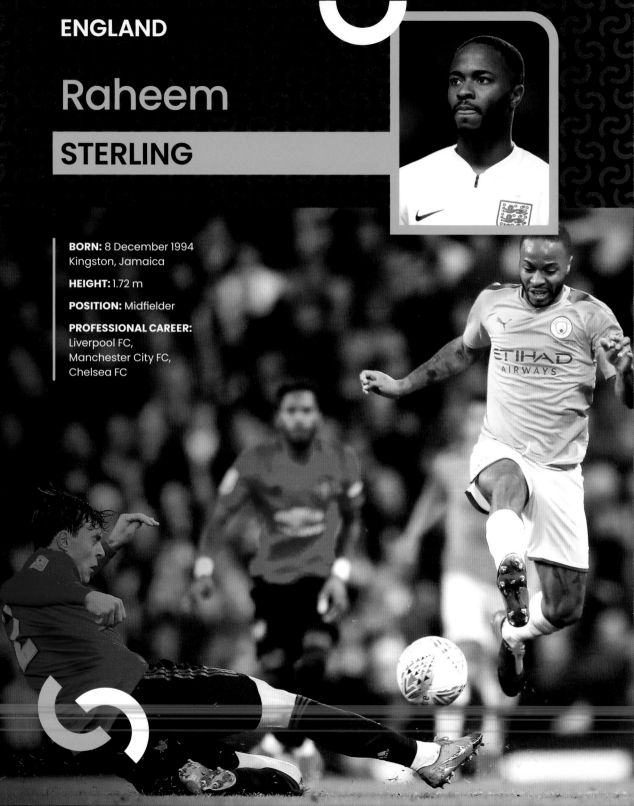

BORN: 8 December 1994
Kingston, Jamaica

HEIGHT: 1.72 m

POSITION: Midfielder

PROFESSIONAL CAREER:
Liverpool FC,
Manchester City FC,
Chelsea FC

I n England Raheem Sterling does not leave many people indifferent and especially not the tabloids, as he is one of the headline writers' favourites. It must be said that the Manchester City striker has given them enough ammunition, with a reputation as a bad boy, tattoos, big cars and his altercation with his teammate Joe Gomez during a national team camp. Nothing is spared of a player whom the gutter press in the United Kingdom have called 'The Hated One' and 'The Hated'.

'I can't do anything about it. I look like a brat,' Sterling lamented. His lively flawed character is perhaps a product of his youth. It's on the rutted bitumen of Maverley, a deprived district of Kingston, the capital of Jamaica, that Raheem Shaquille Sterling first learned football in what was a tumultuous childhood. A few years earlier in this neighbourhood plagued by violence his father was shot dead in cold blood. Raheem was just two years old.

Five years later he was on a plane with his mother and her sister heading for London, everything wasn't all rosy either in the English capital. While his mother worked in a hotel cleaning rooms, Raheem was expelled from primary school. Fortunately, football opened its arms to this promising kid, who never missed a session and controlled his temper.

All the London clubs courted the prodigy. He rejected Arsenal and spent four years with local youth team Alpha & Omega before signing for Queens Park Rangers, then he made a dream move to Liverpool. However, his demons resurfaced, and after close to a century of games for the Reds he refused an extension of his contract to move across to Manchester to link up with Manchester City. This decision, personal as it was, attracted a new wave of criticism from the press.

A year later at the head of the team, Pep Guardiola made The Hated One one of his most vital lieutenants. Trusted by the Catalan, Raheem became a hated player for good this time, by all Premier League defences and opponents of the Three Lions in national team selection! The one his teammate Kevin De Bruyne took for a moron when he arrived at the Sky Blues redeemed himself with the public and the media, which now praises his commitment against racism as well as his outstanding displays.

Sterling returned to the English capital at the start of the 2022–23 season as he linked up with Chelsea.

DID YOU KNOW?

Raheem Sterling is a tattoo lover. One of them, on his right calf, caused controversy across the channel. It represents a submachine gun and shocked the English media, and was a choice that was considered to be totally unacceptable by an association against the bearing of arms. Facing a mountain of criticism, the England international was forced to explain himself. 'When I was two years old my father was killed [by] a gun,' he explained. 'I promised myself I would never touch a gun in my life. I shoot with my right foot, so it has a deeper and still unfinished meaning.'

GERMANY

Marc-André

TER STEGEN

BORN: 30 April 1992
Mönchengladbach,
Germany

HEIGHT: 1.87 m

POSITION: Goalkeeper

PROFESSIONAL CAREER:
Borussia Mönchengladbach,
FC Barcelona

Marc-André ter Stegen, who became the seventh German player to play for FC Barcelona when he joined their powerful squad in the summer of 2014, entered the Catalan monument on tiptoes. The reason for this was he was leaving Germany and entering the unknown.

The young Rhenish stopper had just spent 18 years at Borussia Mönchengladbach, the club of his hometown, which practically adopted him from out of the crib. In April 2011, at just 19 years of age, the intrepid, uninhibited goalkeeper was offered a chance to start in the Bundesliga thanks to the flair of Lucien Favre, then in charge of the Foals – the nickname given to Gladbach players.

Marc-André amazed the local public with his prowess on his line and allowed his team to gain confidence. It was little surprise, then, that when he got a standing ovation on his final game with Borussia 'Marco' cracked and could not hold back the tears.

He arrived in Catalonia with a big challenge: replace Victor Valdés, who had just played 535 games in the Blaugrana jersey. It was, however, a curious first season in the Camp Nou side: he did not play a match in La Liga, as it was the Chilean Claudio Bravo who was favoured for league action. Marco was established in the Spanish Cup side but also, and more importantly, in the Champions League set-up. With a record 13 outings to his credit in the Champions League, the young German goalkeeper lifted the trophy after Barça's 3–1 victory against Juventus.

Despite this flashy career and more than honest beginnings, support for the goalkeeper in the Rhineland was not unanimous. This situation did not panic him, though; time would be his best ally. For his debut with the national team during the 2012–13 season, Marc-André lost in his first three matches: against Switzerland 3–5, Argentina 1–3 and then the United States 3–4. An extremely rare feat for a German international!

He ended up convincing even the most sceptical, and with his calm presence he became an essential piece in the Catalan system and for the national team. At the start of the 2022–23 season he had amassed four La Liga titles and five Copa Del Rey trophies to add to his Champions League gong.

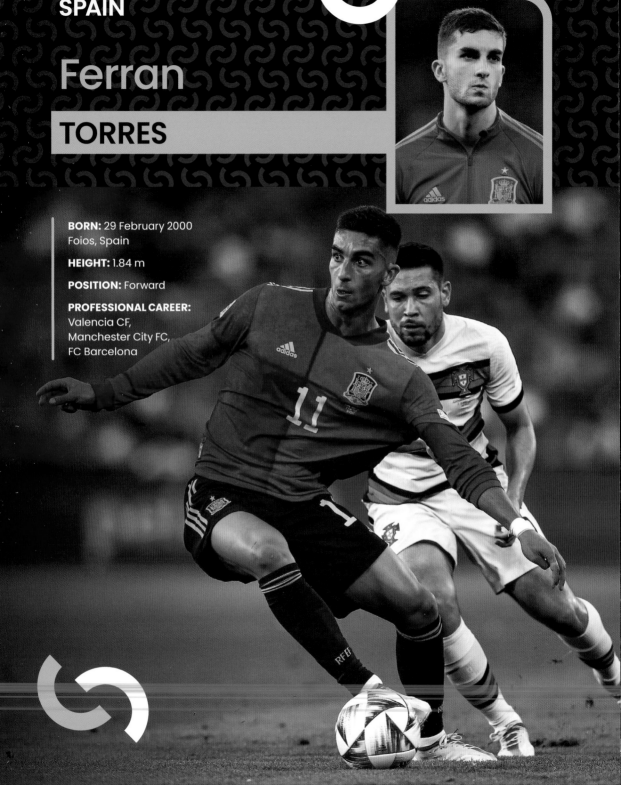

SPAIN

Ferran
TORRES

BORN: 29 February 2000
Foios, Spain

HEIGHT: 1.84 m

POSITION: Forward

PROFESSIONAL CAREER:
Valencia CF,
Manchester City FC,
FC Barcelona

From Paris, Lionel Messi must have choked on seeing the money paid for Ferran Torres by Barça! For €55 million Ferran became the most expensive Spanish signing in the Catalan club's history.

Born into football in Valencia and educated in England by Pep Guardiola in Manchester, Torres arrived in Barcelona with a sign on his back as the announced saviour. Barça was in full reconstruction mode, and fellow Spaniard Xavi arrived on the bench of the club he served in the role of firefighter. On Xavi's list of players to recruit, the City striker was at the very top. This was a return to the country where he made his debut, for Valencia, at only 17 years of age.

He played almost 100 matches in the colours of the Blanquinegros, but the Valencian club was in need of cash and let him slip away for €25 million to Manchester City. The new star of Spanish football scored 16 goals in his first season in the United Kingdom. On the wing life was better, even if his dribbling profile as that of a soloist on one side was undermined by Guardiola.

Repositioned as a false 9 by his coach, Torres adapted and continued his good performances. His versatility and mind proved to give sacred added value, but City had rich problems and a plethora of attackers in his position. The siren call of Barça did the rest. Xavi wanted Ferran and the Spanish striker dreamed of writing the post-Messi history at the Blaugrana club.

In the national team La Roja was counting on him to find his true colours. The youngest player in history to reach 10 goals in the Spanish jersey at 21 years and 192 days, better than Raúl González at 21 years and 277 days or Fernando Torres at 22 years and 79 days, Ferran applied for the position of leader at the forefront of the Spanish attack.

He was the type of goal scorer capable of netting a hat-trick against Germany in a 6–0 win in only his seventh cap. He was the first to achieve this feat against the Germans since England front man Michael Owen had done so in 2001. Any resemblance to the Reds' pocket striker ends there – or perhaps it doesn't. Lifting a Ballon d'Or is not a given for any player, but Ferrán Torres does not rule out anything. There has been the Spain of Fernando Torres, and there is a good chance there will soon be a Ferrán Torres's Spain.

URUGUAY

Federico

VALVERDE

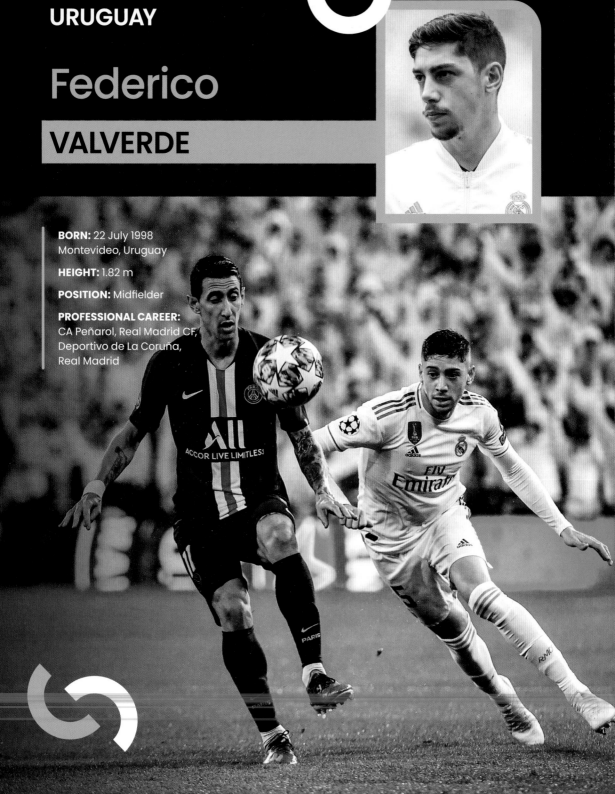

BORN: 22 July 1998
Montevideo, Uruguay

HEIGHT: 1.82 m

POSITION: Midfielder

PROFESSIONAL CAREER:
CA Peñarol, Real Madrid CF,
Deportivo de La Coruña,
Real Madrid

The legend is tenacious and the image sticks in the memory of Federico Santiago Valverde Dipetta. At the start of his life, even when he was barely able to stand up, he was already running after a ball. He joined the Danube Academy in the Uruguayan capital, Montevideo, but even with proper registration the toddler was too small to play official matches. After being introduced to the watching crowd because he looked like a mascot, Little Valverde took off his metaphorical diaper and played anyway in a friendly game in which he scored a goal.

His nickname was profound: 'El niño del panal' (the child in a diaper). He was not even six years of age and already had a good reputation.

Inevitably, after impressing locally the fact that he made the move to Peñarol, the country's flagship club, was no surprise. Despite his introverted side the young man oozed modern football and his rise became dazzling. In the summer of 2016, for just €5 million, Real Madrid sets its sights on the little wonder who enchanted in the middle of the field. A complete player, Valverde is as good at creating openings for others as he is sealing defensive breaches.

Always invaluable in transition phases, he feels at ease everywhere on a field. As for his ability to find penetrative passes, the young Uruguayan has hardly any equivalent. After his debut with the Merengues reserve at La Castilla, Federico went on loan for a season at Deportivo La Coruña to toughen up.

As soon as he returned to the capital, during the 2018–19 season, El Niño immediately seduced Julen Lopetegui and then Santiago Solari, who followed one another on the Real Madrid bench. However, it was during the following term that Valverde took on a new dimension in a squad headed by Zinedine Zidane, a player whom the Uruguayan prodigy worshipped. The French coach had Valverde as the first name on the team sheet when he prepared his roster for matches. The kid had turned the hierarchy, however well established, upside down at Real.

After being awarded the Silver Ball at the 2017 U-20 World Cup, a tournament that convinced Real of his worth, Valverde made his senior debut in August of the same year and went on to become a regular selection for La Celeste.

DID YOU KNOW?

In January 2020 during the Real–Atlético Spanish Super Cup final clash played in Saudi Arabia, Federico Valverde was having a funny evening. After a desperate tackle against Álvaro Morata, the Uruguayan was sent off as the last defender. His team still won, 4–1 on penalties after the game had ended 0–0 after extra time, and Valverde was named as Man of the Match!

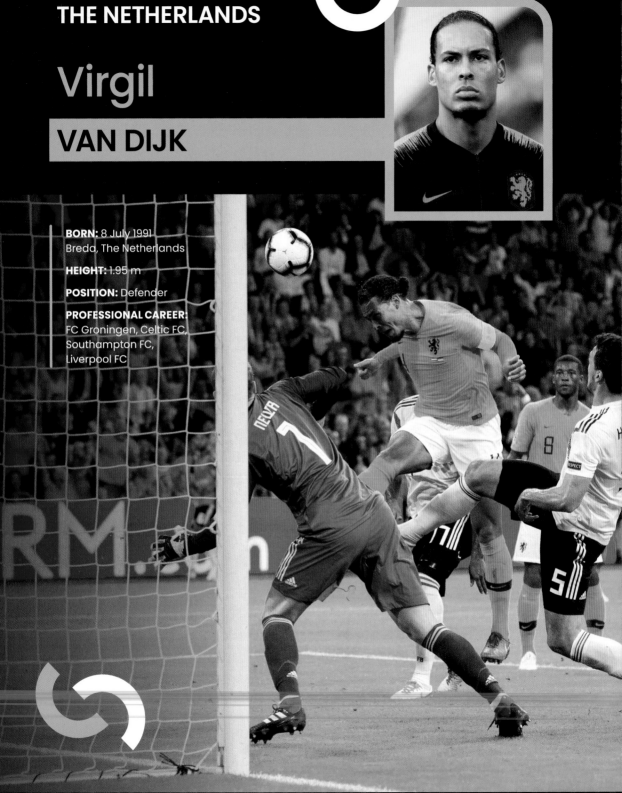

THE NETHERLANDS

Virgil

VAN DIJK

BORN: 8 July 1991
Breda, The Netherlands

HEIGHT: 1.95 m

POSITION: Defender

PROFESSIONAL CAREER:
FC Groningen, Celtic FC,
Southampton FC,
Liverpool FC

With only a few titles gleaned in Scotland, Virgil van Dijk came to the Reds to fill his cupboard with trophies, and he came so close in the Premier League in May 2019 when his Liverpool side went neck and neck with Manchester City in the title race. With the Citizens racking up 98 points to seal the title against Liverpool's 97, the pill was hard to swallow. Fortunately, the epilogue in the Champions League had a much more favourable outcome for the Dutchman and his teammates, winners of the final against Tottenham Hotspur.

When he arrived at Anfield in the winter of 2018, van Dijk did not imagine that his signing would become a political issue. The cost of the fee was a bone of contention and especially with José Mourinho, then coach of Manchester United. 'Our competitors are buying defenders at the cost of attackers,' Mourinho bemoaned. His German counterpart at Anfield, Jürgen Klopp, warmed the spirits of van Dijk when he replied to the Portuguese coach's grumbles. 'We don't set the prices; it's the market,' was Klopp's rejoinder.

Far from all these controversies, Virgil quickly melded into the Liverpool collective. In his role as a towering centre back 'Vig' has few equals. He works standing up, never throwing himself at the feet of an adversary, and anticipates actions before they take place. Obviously, with his stature his aerial game borders on perfection. With an excellent passing range, the Dutchman does not hesitate to take risks to find his attackers.

The only question from Reds fans when he arrived at Liverpool was his perceived inexperience. His career up to that point had taken in Groningen in his homeland, Glasgow Celtic and Southampton, decent clubs but not of the stature of Liverpool. Charismatic and determined, van Dijk adapted well to European evenings and high-tempo encounters against the English Big Five, leading his team to the title in 2019–20 and banishing memories of the year before.

Since his debut with the Netherlands in 2014 he has been a mainstay of the Oranje defence and their return to prominence in international football, and the colossus of Breda is no stranger to the Dutch revival. It was van Dijk who, in equalising in stoppage time against Germany – the match ending 2–2 – who sent Ronald Koeman's team into the four-team Nations League finals at the expense of France in 2019.

DID YOU KNOW?

For €84 million, Virgil van Dijk signed with Liverpool on 27 December 2017. Transferred from Southampton, the Dutchman thus became at that time the most expensive defender in the history of football. In the standings he was ahead of two Frenchmen: Aymeric Laporte and Benjamin Mendy, both recruited by Manchester City. Like some of the stars of Dutch football such as Frank Rijkaard or Ruud Gullit, the Liverpool defender is of Surinamese origin through his mother.

FRANCE

Raphaël

VARANE

BORN: 25 April 1993
Lille, France

HEIGHT: 1.91 m

POSITION: Defender

PROFESSIONAL CAREER:
Racing Club de Lens,
Real Madrid,
Manchester United FC

I t seems a long time ago that Raphaël Varane was found to be too nice and too weak to wear the blue jersey. The 'Pearl from the North' has established himself as a pillar of the team, a changing-room leader and a boss on the field. At Manchester United, as at Real Madrid and the French team, the native of Lille is finally the world-class defender everyone expected. Varane turned professional at the age of 17 at Racing Club de Lens, and by age 18 was a member of the Real Madrid changing room, was captain of the French side at age 21 and a quadruple European champion with the Merengues at age 25. Varane is a model of success.

Never one to talk up his own game, Varane's interventions on and off the field are thoughtful. On this somewhat overrated football planet the adopted Mancunian is a little like the ideal son-in-law who everyone unanimously likes in all circumstances. If you look carefully you might find a small defect: there are many who think Varane lacks aggressiveness in his game, and the duel he lost against the German Mats Hummels, who eliminated Les Bleus at the Maracanã, is the perfect illustration. France was out of the Brazilian World Cup 2014 and the Nationalmannschaft jumped to the title.

This action often haunted Varane and his detractors did not hesitate to remind him, but four years later he had the opportunity to take his revenge. It was him this time who jumped higher than all the Uruguayan defence to catapult a firm header into the back of the net. The Blues, in white that day facing the band of Suárez, were well on their way to their second star and all knew what they owed Varane. He became a natural leader and an insurmountable wall in all circumstances, a defender who was never overly physical and always so technical but an intractable man marker. Attackers of the World Cup in Russia learned this the hard way.

A swathe of trophies with Real Madrid, three La Liga titles to go alongside four UEFA Champions League triumphs and four FIFA Club world cups were just the topping on a magnificent time in Spain. It was, perhaps, somewhat surprising that Madrid, after the departure of Zinedine Zidane, allowed Varane to move to England and take up the new challenge in Manchester. It's one he met head on, scoring his first United goal against Brentford in May 2022 and becoming a vital cog in new manager Erik ten Hag's Manchester United.

VARANE

DID YOU KNOW?

Raphaël Varane preferred to revise his baccalaureate rather than respond immediately to Zinedine Zidane, an adviser to Florentino Pérez, who offered him the opportunity to sign at Real Madrid. That didn't stop him from signing for Real once he had his diploma in his pocket and to begin to stack up the trophies with the Merengues.

ITALY

Marco

VERRATTI

BORN: 5 November 1992
Pescara, Italy

HEIGHT: 1.65 m

POSITION: Midfielder

PROFESSIONAL CAREER:
Delfino Pescara,
Paris Saint-Germain FC,
Al-Arabi FC

At times like these he really can't deny his origins: he is Italian to the very end. When Marco Verratti approached a referee in the middle of a match it was rarely for a chat about last night's movie. By walking the talk the 'toddler of Pescara' led with his stock in trade: 'But, Monsieur l'Arbitrator . . . I can't believe my eyes . . .' It is the dark side of his character that he is a collector of yellow cards despite his eternal allure as an ingenuous teenager.

It would be too simplistic to summarise the impact of the jewel of Abruzzo on this plain annoying detail. On the tactical side he is, above all, a godsend for a coach. In the heart of the game Verratti is a formidable tackler, but his talent is not limited to this aspect. Valuable in moving the ball, he is also an excellent first-line passer. His precision in the timing of his pass is a boon for his attackers.

Observers constantly remind us that without the Italian PSG is not the same. Some say he has a holy influence. When he landed at the foot of the Eiffel Tower in 2012 it was with the seasoned Zlatan Ibrahimović, Ezequiel Lavezzi and Thiago Silva. It quickly became apparent that even if the boy was still unknown he already appeared to be an indispensable piece in the puzzle put in place by this version of PSG.

Champions of France again in 2020 for the seventh time, the Italian did falter alongside his team during the crucial Champions League meeting against Manchester United. It was an anomaly for this pure talent, who has not yet reached his full potential – and to think that little Marco almost never turned pro.

A knee injury just before he fully matured that deprived him of an entire season on the field for Pescara was a blow. When fit he was straight back in the workforce of the Biancazzurri, and he actively participated in the rise of the club of his heart. Marco Verratti does not forget his origins but that has not stopped him from falling in love with Paris, the place where his son Tommaso was born, and he has now mastered French. That, then, is perfect for when it gets tense during a match at the Parc des Princes or elsewhere.

After winning 30 major trophies during his glittering career in Paris, Verratti upped sticks at the end of the 2022–23 season, Al-Arabi securing his coveted signature for the 2023–24 Saudi Pro League campaign.

VERRATTI

DID YOU KNOW?

A youth at his former club of Pescara until the age of 19, Marco Verratti never played in the elite of Italian competition. When he left his country to sign for PSG in 2012 his club had just moved up to Serie A and therefore Marco never played at the top level of the Italian championship, which is extremely rare for an Italian international. For almost a decade since then clubs such as Juventus, Milan and Napoli have dreamed of recovering the little 'Owl' from France.

Dušan

VLAHOVIĆ

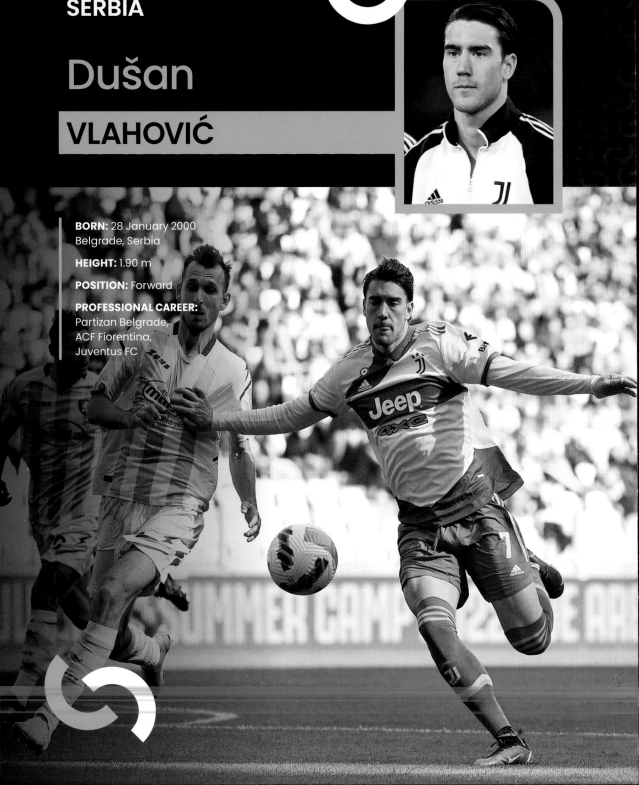

BORN: 28 January 2000
Belgrade, Serbia

HEIGHT: 1.90 m

POSITION: Forward

PROFESSIONAL CAREER:
Partizan Belgrade,
ACF Fiorentina,
Juventus FC

The Old Lady did not hesitate to break her piggy bank to snap up the striker, spending nearly €80 million in the middle of winter 2021 – a record for the mid-season transfer window. It is true that the goal scorer's figures were enough to turn the heads of the Juventus board in Turin: 49 goals and 8 assists in 108 games at Fiorentina, which ranked him as a serious Serie A striker. Now the Serbian was installed at the top of the Bianconeri attack, with the famous number 7 on his back and in the position once inhabited by Cristiano Ronaldo.

Born on 28 January 2000, Vlahović twice offered himself a birthday in the form of a transfer that changed his life. On the day he turned 22 the imposing Serbian striker signed for Juventus, as he had done four years earlier, leaving Partizan Belgrade – the club that had become too small for him – that same day. His destination was Tuscany and Fiorentina.

Before adopting Italy as his new lifestyle, the centre forward was stacking up the goals at school from the age of 10 in his native Serbia. The two big clubs of the country were not long in coming to learn about the phenomenon everyone had tried to attract. Red Star Belgrade pressed hard, but little Dušan finally opted for their rival: Partizan of Belgrade. At only 16 years and 22 days of age he made his debut in the Serbian league. Two months later he became the youngest to score a goal in the whole history of the club.

Dušan barely had time to make a name for himself in his own country before 'Fio' knocked on the door. The Viola poured just under €2 million into his signing, seeing Vlahović as the man to lead them out of their relative mire and restore the image of the club. Nicknamed the 'Batistuta of the 21st century' by the Viola fans in tribute to the prolific Argentinian, Dušan as the all-time top scorer of Fiorentina became a safe bet.

The attention of the big European clubs was becoming more and more pressing and Fiorentina were anxious to agree on a contract extension. It was a story of big money between a player ready to leave for free and a club keen to recover some sort of recompense in the event of a transfer. The Florentine president Rocco Commisso cried foul in the press, ensuring that Vlahović didn't walk away for nothing. Juventus got their man, but for a princely sum.

DID YOU KNOW?

Dušan Vlahović did not experience the war in Bosnia, but he was born there at the end of the conflict. Like many families in the former Yugoslavia, his own mourned the loss of a close member during those dark years: his older brother died during the armed conflict. As a tribute, Dušan got his brother's name tattooed on his right hand.

VLAHOVIĆ

THE NETHERLANDS

Georginio
WIJNALDUM

BORN: 11 November 1990
Rotterdam,
The Netherlands

HEIGHT: 1.75 m

POSITION: Midfielder

PROFESSIONAL CAREER:
Feyenoord Rotterdam,
PSV Eindhoven,
Newcastle United FC,
Liverpool FC,
Paris Saint-Germain FC,
AS Roma, Al-Ettifaq FC

The Swiss army knife is actually a thin Dutch blade. A versatile player and a specialist in box to box, 'Gini' Wijnaldum is an excellent watchdog in midfield, always biting the calves of his opponents. But this old striker who trained at Sparta Rotterdam did not lose his sense of purpose. Of Surinamese origin, the Dutchman proved it during that magical Anfield night of 7 May 2019 during the Champions League semi-final second leg against FC Barcelona. 'Wijnaldinho' became with the Belgian striker Divock Origi, both scorers of a double, the heroes of the evening.

Number 5 entered the legend of Liverpool. While coach Jürgen Klopp left his 'man with three lungs' on the bench at the start of the match, it took an injury to the Scotsman Andrew Robertson to see Wijnaldum finally enter the stage. Hungry for success, as soon as he came on and perhaps with a point to prove, Georginio showed character and got over his nerves quickly, terrorising the Catalan defence.

A humble start for Wijnaldum began when, not even 17 years old and still living at home with his grandmother, he played in the Eredivisie, the Dutch League 1, in the jersey of Feyenoord. During his childhood the round ball did not really interest him: he saw himself rather as an acrobat or a gymnast, and his flexibility was an asset that was transferrable on the first training grounds he strode across. The supporters fell in love with this boy full of rage who appeared to be made of rubber and had a famous mane of hair.

In 2011 Gini left the great Dutch port for PSV Eindhoven and earned his first cap in the famous orange jersey of the Dutch national team. Then, aged 24, he took the plunge and joined the English Premier League. In October 2015 with Newcastle he allowed himself the luxury of being more selfish and scored a hat-trick against Norwich City. The story ended painfully, though, with the Magpies relegated at the end of the 2015–16 season.

Upon his arrival at Liverpool Wijnaldum was repositioned as a midfielder by Jürgen Klopp, although one still full of flair. In 2021 the ex-captain of the Oranje joined Paris Saint-Germain but things were more often worse than better in the French capital, and he began the 2022–23 season on loan to Roma in Serie A. He eventually joined the long list of European expats to land in Saudi Arabia, in Wijnaldum's case his destination being Al-Ettifaq.

DID YOU KNOW?

His half-brother Rajiv van La Parra, a right winger by trade, played in Ligue 1. After growing up like his eldest brother at Feyenoord, Dutchman van La Parra was recruited in 2008 to the Malherbe stadium in Caen. With just 20 matches in three seasons for the Norman club he returned to the country of his birth, signing for SC Heerenveen. Georginio Wijnaldum has another brother, Giliano Wijnaldum, who plays as a left back at Willem II Tilburg.

COLOMBIA

Duván

ZAPATA

BORN: 1 April 1991
Padilla, Columbia

HEIGHT: 1.86 m

POSITION: Striker

PROFESSIONAL CAREER:
América de Cali,
Estudiantes de La Plata,
SSC Napoli, Udinese
Calcio, UC Sampdoria,
Atalanta BC, Torino FC
(loan)

The son did not want to wear gloves. With great assurance, he decided not to follow the recommendations of his father, who dreamed of making it as a goalkeeper. Duván Esteban Zapata was eyeing the other end of the field while he spent his time playing football in the narrow streets of the Cordoba district. With disconcerting agility, the young Zapata was both facetious and energetic.

After joining the America School, the most exclusive club in Cali, from the age of six, Zapata rose through the ranks. At the gates of the first team 10 years later, he signed professional forms with the Colombian Red Devils. After appearing in the U-20 World Cup, contested in 2011 at home – Les Cafeteros were knocked out in the quarter finals – Duván went to Argentina after being recruited by Estudiantes. In three seasons on that side of La Plata 'El Toro', a nickname linked to his robustness, turned into a regular and opportunistic goal scorer.

Such potential quickly caught the eye of European recruiters. West Ham United appeared to be in pole position to land the phenomenal Colombian, but the London club could not manage to get him a work permit. Finally, in August 2013 Napoli welcomed young Zapata, who had received good advice from his cousin Cristian, then a defender at AC Milan. Napoli was convinced that Duván had all the assets to succeed in the Italian Serie A.

Napoli's coach Rafael Benítez praised the qualities of his new striker. From his debut in the Champions League, the 'Caleño' distinguished himself by scoring against Olympique Marseille. Everything seemed ideal, but after a successful first season at the foot of Vesuvius Duván Zapata became disillusioned: the Spaniard Benítez had confined him to a place on the bench.

The South American striker agreed to become a luxury nomad in Italy and was lent in quick succession to Udinese, Sampdoria and then Atalanta. On the Bergamo side Zapata found his feet and quickly became a revelation. On a personal note he had found a home from a sporting perspective, and he was an instrumental part of the Lombard team that thrilled the crowds and millions watching on television in the Champions League. The Colombian brought his experience with him, and after soon being joined by compatriot Luis Muriel he helped hoist the club to the heights of European football. Long live Zapata!

DID YOU KNOW?

After a tussle between Milan and Atalanta in January 2021, the verbal exchange between Zlatan Ibrahimović and Duván Zapata did the rounds on social networks. Exasperated by a dive by the Swede, the Colombian said to him, 'You cannot finish a match without a penalty!' 'Ibra' coolly replied: 'I have scored more goals than the number of matches you have played in your career!' Zapata had the last laugh that day, the Colombian scoring a goal as Atalanta inflicted a memorable 3–0 defeat on Zlatan and his team.

Photographic credits